REST IN PEACE?

Rest in Peace?

A light-hearted look at the After-life

CYRIL BLACKSHAW

Best Wishes
Cyril Blackshaw

SERENDIPITY

Copyright © Cyril Blackshaw, 2004

First published in 2004 by
Serendipity
Suite 530
37 Store Street
Bloomsbury
London

All rights reserved
Unauthorised duplication
contravenes existing laws

British Library Cataloguing-in-Publication data
A catalogue record for this book is available from the British Library

ISBN 1 84394 079 5

Printed and bound by Alden Press, Oxford

Contents

Chapter

1.	Meet the Family	1
2.	The Best Days of Our Lives	4
3.	Jet Set, Ready, Go!	12
4.	The Last Days	31
5.	Why Me?	43
6.	Secret Lemonade Drinker	56
7.	Save the Last Séance For Me	64
8.	Who You Gonna Call – Ghost Buster!	70
9.	Children, Too? No, Andrew Please!	82
10.	Commuter Rail Crash	90
11.	Travel Broadens the Mind	100
12.	Memories	123
13.	Ghost – The Movie?	132
14.	Voices From Beyond the Grave!	141
15.	Jet Lag on a Higher Plane	152
16.	Man's Best Friend	160
17.	Paradise Cruise Liners	169
18.	Midsummer Madness	195

To my patient wife, Christine, for all her arduous proof-reading and her understanding, love and commitment

John King and John Beverage, whose book about Princess Diana removed my 'blinkered' vision of life, and caused me to research the true 'meaning of life'.

CHAPTER ONE

Meet the Family

Arthur James Coney was a quiet sort of man, 55 years old, loved his wife and two grown up sons and lived in a little semi-detached house in a quiet cul-de-sac in the quiet part of a medium sized town in the Midlands.

As a young boy he was forced into an apprenticeship by his dominant father and became a certified gas installation engineer. His father had anticipated the rise in the use of natural gas and the change from coal heating, as he was always at the Working Men's Club where he drank with the likes of coal miners and other interesting parties from local government and services. There was more coal mined around that table of beer glasses than at any pit in the country, and so many correct decisions were made on behalf of the government that would truly benefit the populace. He wanted his son to have a job that would always be there, long after the mines had closed and one that would stand him in good stead for the whole of his working life. And you always need a plumber at least! Although he was out of work, he still kept a watchful eye on the world and its comings and goings, listening to the nightly news on the television and cursing the present government for its actions, gathering fuel for the nightly debates around the beer tables.

Jimmy, as everyone called him, had worked hard over the years and now had the job of a foreman on the lines, where he took charge of laying miles of pipes to new housing estates, and repairing or replacing the old stuff. Organising a gang of men was easy, even for an emergency during the early hours. It was stressing work but he loved it, and he was given a company van full of special equipment for testing and finding pipe-work. If it was anything to do with gas piping, he knew all about it.

At 55, he was celebrating thirty-four years in the job; a milestone in terms of pension rights, and by now the prospect of early retirement was not such a bad idea. He had plans to pay off the mortgage, get the house in order and probably take a well-earned holiday in America. His wife Hazel had always set her heart on going to Florida, but it never seemed to happen. There was always something to hinder the holiday plans, like, no one on call-out except Jimmy, everyone's booked the same weeks that Jimmy wanted and he is left to mind the office and run the job. Well, he is the best man to run the place. Jimmy worked every hour he could, sometimes too many for one man. A team would be called out in the middle of the night to repair a leak, and whilst they were unloading the truck, Jimmy would be there to locate the exact position for them. This would be after he had been at work from nine till five, or whatever time he finished. Hazel often told him that he was working too much and that if he didn't slow down a bit he would end up having a heart attack and die. Jimmy was 'the company'.

Nothing happened without Jimmy being involved, including after hours meetings and Union involvement, to make sure his teams of men were well looked after by the company.

Hazel had married Jimmy when he was about to finish college at the age of twenty-two, after courting him for three years and she had had no other boyfriends. Jimmy had been the only child in his family and Hazel was his only girlfriend. They met at the Working Men's Club where his father spent most of his time, and yes, Hazel was the daughter of his father's best friend. They seemed to hit it off from the start and the relationship grew into a good marriage, blessed with two fine sons, Martin and Gerry. A well-paid job took care of all the household bills with some left over for savings, and the ongoing threat of a holiday abroad. Well, it was all the time off he could get to spend a week in a caravan at the seaside, or a hotel in London on a "theatre break" special. Even then, his mobile phone was constantly by his side and regularly rang in the most awkward places. Hazel was a good cook and housekeeper. She was a brilliant wife and mother, and it was only the long hours that Jimmy put in at work that caused a few minor rows in the house. She realised that he was trying to earn as much as he could to better his pension at this stage in his life, and that this would be beneficial when he did retire, if he ever did. Life without the gas industry was something that she could never imagine, because it had been the only thing that Jimmy had ever done, and the only thing he ever talked about!

Martin, the eldest son, was in banking. At thirty years old he was a deputy manager at the local bank and was reaching the time to move up to the top position. He had a wife and two young girls, and a lovely home in a small village on the outskirts of town. It was a beautiful house, with perfect lawns, and new cars on the driveway.

Gerry was twenty-five, the travelling type. He had no ties except a few past relationships that had failed, and would take up any challenge that was on offer. He was always jetting off to some third world country to help the starving, or plant rice fields, or help out in some war-torn region. If some disaster took place in some far off land, he was there. This was funded by his love of photography. His pictures and articles were bought by many of the national newspapers. Once a week, Hazel would have a phone call from some unknown place in the world, and it would be Gerry, just to see that everything was all right at home, and to assure his worrying mother that he was still safe. She would always say a little prayer each night for his safety, though she didn't profess to be a "churchly" person. When he returned home she could relax, and his room was always kept in fine fettle ready for him. That was the time when she could feed him up and make sure he got the nourishment that he had more than likely missed.

Hazel used to bring home some brochures from the travel agent, and try to interest Jimmy in a holiday in the sun. She'd be half way through convincing him of how nice it would be when the phone would ring, and Jimmy would have to go off to sort out a problem at some site or other. The brochures usually ended up in the bin because they had become out of date, by something like a year!

If they could stay together for a couple of hours and have a barbecue in the evening, or a weekend without a phone call, that was like a holiday for Hazel.

CHAPTER TWO

The Best Days of Our Lives

One day Jimmy came home a little earlier than usual and called to Hazel as he came into the house. This was not normal, and Hazel thought the worst, that something was drastically wrong. Had he been injured? Had he been to hospital or something?

Jimmy sat down at the dining table and pulled out some sheets of paper, which he began to read to himself.

"Hazel," he said, "for a while now, I've been hearing rumours about a company taking over ours, and there are going to be some good deals coming up for redundancy and early retirement."

Hazel was speechless.

"How on earth will you manage to LIVE without that damn phone and those damn gas pipes?" said Hazel incredulously, once she had got over the shock of his statement.

Jimmy looked in amazement at his wife's blunt question. "What do you mean? I only work to keep a roof over our heads and food on the table."

"Work," retorted Hazel, "you've practically lived there all the time I've known you, and the family always came second to those gas pipes! You eat, sleep and breathe gas pipes!"

"Well, perhaps you're right, dear, but it's all going to change, because after all my years of living the job, I am now too old!"

"Too old? At 58 you should be wearing the director's suit and driving his big Jaguar!" replied Hazel. "Anyway, who's told you that you're too old? You know more about those pipes and how to run that company than anyone in Britain!" Although she hated being second to the job, she was now defending her husband's credibility.

"This little piece of paper that suggests I take advantage of the new company's redundancy and pension offer," replied Jimmy in a strange sort of "I'm very, very interested" kind of voice.

Hazel sat down at the table alongside him, and glanced at the paperwork. "This is ridiculous, Jimmy, they can't get rid of you! Who will do your job?" snapped Hazel, in his defence again.

"That won't matter to me, will it? 'Cause I will be jetting off to America, Orlando even, and relaxing in the sunshine with my dear wife, who hasn't seen enough of me all these years," said Jimmy, with a wry grin on his face.

"What!" said Hazel, startled.

"What you and I need, my dear, is a month in the States, where there are no pipes or mobile phones for us to worry about," said Jimmy, as he pulled out two airline tickets from the inside pocket of his jacket. He laid them on the table in front of Hazel.

Hazel went berserk! She screamed and cried and hugged and kissed as Jimmy whirled her around the dining room.

"Wait a minute!" said Hazel, coming back to earth with a bump, "do you mean to say that you are going to accept ..?"

Jimmy cut her short. "I've seen this coming for months, and I've made all my plans to grab what I can and get the hell out. I filled out the forms a week ago and they came straight back the next day, accepted. I couldn't believe it. I thought they would never get rid of me, after all my years and hard work. It just goes to show how much they think of people who do their best, day in and day out, day and night, for years, and then they just write a cheque and you're a nobody. I'm officially on the scrap heap!"

"They wrote you a cheque?" enquired Hazel quietly.

"Yeah, look at this, £75,000 in your hand, a pension every week and good bye Jimmy!"

Hazel grabbed the cheque from Jimmy's hand. A squeal of delight filled the room, no, the whole house. "So when does all this happen, Jimmy?" she asked excitedly.

"At 3 o'clock today," replied Jimmy.

"What! You're already finished?" asked Hazel, hardly able to contain her joy.

"Yep! That's me done for the rest of our lives," replied Jimmy. "Now, what about getting some accommodation sorted out in Orlando, eh?"

Hazel stood motionless, staring at the cheque. "I can't wait to tell the boys," she said as her excitement took over again, "what will they say?"

"Never mind them," said Jimmy, "it's going to be a new life, a new start for the two of us from now on. We're going to go places and see things that we've never seen before or thought existed. And don't bother to get the dinner ready, we're dining out tonight as a special celebration."

He picked up the phone and booked a table for 7.30 p.m. at one of the best restaurants in town. The booking was for six people, as he'd already phoned the boys, and even managed to get hold of Gerry who just happened to be back in the country, with a girl in tow. But he didn't tell Hazel that they would all be there, that would be a surprise.

On the way home from his last day at work, and not having the van any more, he decided to catch the bus as he used to do in the early days. The bus didn't come for over twenty minutes, so Jimmy started to walk, probably to the next stop. On the way he passed a garage showroom where they had a special deal going on for "no trade-ins." Jimmy didn't have a car; he went everywhere in the work's van because he only went places when he was working! His daughter-in-law took Hazel to the supermarket once a week, Jimmy always walked to the local pub, so that he wasn't far away if the mobile rang, so he had never had any use for a car. There, in the corner of the garage forecourt was a brand new hatchback, fitted with number plates, taxed and ready to go.

"That would be just big enough for the two of us," thought Jimmy. He walked in to ask about it, and a salesman came over to him. Apparently, the person who had ordered the car had just lost his job, so it was all ready for the road, but back on sale again.

"It has only delivery mileage," said the salesman, "in fact, it's only been driven around the forecourt once or twice for cleaning and checking out."

The bright blue car had caught Jimmy's eye, but he was quite a shrewd man when it came to parting with his money. He had quite a lot saved up in the bank, and now he'd just been given what he called a "pools win" as well. (In the 1960s, if you won £75,000 on the pools you were like a millionaire!)

The salesman knocked some money off the original price, and gave Jimmy a discount for not having a car to part-exchange, and Jimmy drove it home.

By the time all the excitement had sunk in with Hazel, and they were ready to go for the meal, she suddenly realised that they hadn't booked a taxi!

Jimmy smiled as he opened the front door and calmly said to her, "I'll have the time to take you shopping in the future, won't I?"

As the outside security light lit up the front of the house, Hazel saw the brand new car standing on the driveway.

Was there any limit to the number of surprises that Jimmy had for her? No, not yet, as she didn't know that their two sons and their women were also meeting them at the restaurant.

Hazel loved the car, and was quite giddy with excitement all the way to the restaurant. She said that she would like to take driving lessons, and Jimmy agreed. Well, it would be handy for trips to the pub when it was raining.

At the restaurant, the manager greeted them and he showed them to their table. Waiting for them was Martin and his wife and Gerry and a young girl called Marie that he had just been working with in China. Hazel was overcome with happiness and had to sit down. Then she went to each one of them and gave them a hug and a kiss. She looked at Jimmy. "You crafty old sod!" she said with a big smile.

"Have less of the old," replied Jimmy, "that's only my occupational title!"

Through the evening Jimmy told the boys about his plans to whisk their mother off to strange and wonderful places, starting with the one that she had always longed to go to, Orlando.

"When are you going, Mum?" asked Gerry.

"Oh, I don't know, your father's got the tickets though," she replied.

"Well, what's the date on tickets?" asked Martin.

"Date? Do the tickets have a date on them?" asked Hazel, looking at each of them for an answer. "Jimmy, what's the date on those tickets?"

"They are for a week on Saturday," replied Jimmy calmly.

"What! A week on THIS Saturday! You must be mad! How can we just up and go that quickly? What about ..."

Jimmy cut her short again for the second time that evening, and said, "Of course we can, there's nothing to stop us even going to the airport from this table and jumping on a plane to anywhere in the world."

Hazel couldn't grasp the situation, this was totally not Jimmy Coney the gas pipe man, who could never go anywhere.

The boys laughed at the expression on their mother's face, the shock, the realisation that Jimmy was doing things that they, or rather she had wanted to do for years.

"It won't take you long to shove a few things in a suitcase, dear," said Jimmy, "and what we forget to take, we'll buy new when we get to America. I've read all those brochures that you used to bring home, without you knowing, and I think we might just pick up a few bargains over there. If we can get a deal on some dollars from the holiday shop, it'll be cheap shopping."

"Pinch me," said Hazel to Martin, "or is this some alien that's got into your father's body? All the years I've known this man, he has never talked like this. Martin, is he doing the right thing, or is he going out of his mind?"

Martin answered immediately, "Mum, it's what you've always dreamed about, and now that Dad's working life is finished, you can spend as much time together as you want, go where you want, do what you want, have what you've always wanted."

"Mum, it's a great opportunity to see the world, like I have," said Gerry, "though not in the places that I get to. Travelling is a fantastic experience. You see things that you never believed possible. Go to America and go to the large resorts like Disney and Epcot, you'll be totally amazed! Enjoy every moment, and you've got the means now to be totally happy and carefree."

This was all too much for her to take in, but the idea was growing on her.

At the end of the evening they all met back at Jimmy and Hazel's house. Jimmy showed Martin the paperwork for his pension, which would be paid directly into the branch where Martin worked. Jimmy felt secure with that, as Martin would be able to keep an eye on it for him. The mortgage on their house had been paid off a few years earlier, so there were no worries there.

The next day, Hazel began the search through her wardrobe to find what she could pack for America. Most of the clothes she had were quite well worn and out of date; after all, they had never gone out much while Jimmy was working.

Jimmy suggested a shopping trip to one of those large malls, like the Lakeside Centre at London, where they could both get some really good stuff to take on holiday. So the next day, they went to London and shopped till they dropped.

"This is what we are going to do in the future," said Jimmy, "enjoy ourselves and have the rest of our lives without any worries. Do you think you will get used to the idea eventually?"

"I will, but will you?" replied Hazel.

"Hungry?" asked Jimmy.

"Yes, I think I'm quite ready for something to eat," said Hazel.

"When we get off the motorway I know a nice little pub where we can eat, and it's not far from home," said Jimmy, as they approached the junction that he wanted.

The usual end to any day for Hazel was cooking a meal for Jimmy when he was due in from work. And that also meant waiting for him to eventually arrive at all hours, depending upon what the current situation was with some pipe problem. Now, all that was changed, and here they were, together, popping into a nice roadside pub for a meal. Sometimes she felt like she had to pinch the skin on her arm, just to make sure that she wasn't dreaming all this, and waking to find it all the same as it had been for the last thirty-three years.

Early on the Saturday morning, Martin came round with his big car, and drove them to the airport. Hazel was aghast at the size of it, and was absolutely thrilled as they waved goodbye to Martin, and boarded the aeroplane for Florida. Although she had never flown before, her excitement quelled any fears and Jimmy was beside her. He had never flown either, but he didn't show any kind of fear, only excitement and contentment knowing that he had made Hazel very happy. There was still the love and romance between them and it had been stifled for a long while by gas pipes.

"We should have done this years ago," said Jimmy, as the plane taxied to the runway.

"Well, it's not for want of me trying to get through to you!" replied Hazel with a smile, "perhaps I should have phoned you on your mobile and pretended there was a gas leak at the airport."

Jimmy chuckled, and then they both looked at each other as the engines roared, and the plane shot off down the runway and up into the bright, blue sky.

The holiday lasted four weeks, which seemed to pass quickly as they crammed as much as possible into every moment. They enjoyed some forgotten moments too, as the romance in their marriage came to the forefront once again. On their return, anyone could see that the long-awaited holiday had done so much good to them both. When Martin met them at the airport, they were virtually glowing with love. Tales of America lasted for weeks with Hazel, who couldn't help but talk about the holiday to everyone she met.

One day, about two months later, Jimmy came back from the pub one lunchtime and said to Hazel, "Have you seen what they're advertising on the window of the holiday shop? Two weeks in Greece for £99 each, but you've got to fly there on Friday."

Hazel looked at him with a smile. "Shall I pack the cases while you get the tickets sorted out?"

Life was certainly different in the Coney household. Hazel said to Catherine, Martin's wife, that it was like courting Jimmy all over again but this time there was nothing to get in the way. No job, no gas pipes, no phone.

That first year of retirement saw the pair of them go to America, Greece, Spain and France. But France was only a day-trip to buy some cigarettes and booze. As Jimmy said, when you're retired you've got time to do these things.

CHAPTER THREE

Jet Set, Ready, Go!

The financial side of things stayed very stable under the watchful eye of Martin at the bank. The money was carefully invested and the returns that it earned meant that there was no need to worry about money at all. Then there was the pension coming in every month.

Hazel took driving lessons and passed her test after two failed attempts. Now she could drive to the supermarket and do the shopping, sometimes calling round for Catherine and taking her along too. It was also handy when they went out for a meal or a drink, as Jimmy tended to like to drink more than Hazel could. But she didn't mind in the least, as it gave her a chance to drive the lovely little blue car.

One day, they had a phone call from someone in Afghanistan, who was travelling with a camera crew to the war-torn areas of that country. Jimmy recognised him as Peter, a close friend of Gerry's who had gone off with him on several jaunts to capture on film the disasters and heartaches of the world. There wasn't much time to speak, and Jimmy could hear gunfire in the background.

"Mr Coney, can you hear me?"

"Hello, is that Peter?"

"Yes! Listen! Me and Gerry are filming here in Afghanistan and we've just been bombed out!"

"Peter is Gerry with you?"

"Yes, ..." the conversation was cut short by a loud bang and then some gunfire.

"Peter are you still there?" shouted Jimmy down the phone, as Hazel hung onto every word she could hear from his side.

"Hello, Mr Coney," came the reply.

"Peter, we're still here, are you alright?"

Silence for two or three seconds seemed like an hour, then Peter came back on.

"Mr Coney, Gerry has been taken to a make-shift hospital near Kabul, but he's not dying, he's just been badly wounded."

"Badly wounded?" shouted Jimmy. "What do you mean, 'badly wounded,' Peter?"

There were another two or three seconds of silence before Peter came back.

"Sorry for the break up, but I'm on a field telephone. He's been shot in the arm, and to make things even worse, it's his drinking arm too!"

Jimmy realised that the little bit of comedy was to try and reassure them that he wasn't too badly injured. Jimmy repeated everything immediately to Hazel.

"What can we do from this end, Peter?" shouted Jimmy.

"Get in touch with the TV station at Nottingham and ask them to get us out of here as fast as they can. We've made it to a make-shift hospital near Kabul." There was some more gunfire and a loud explosion, and then the connection went dead.

Jimmy looked at Hazel and she looked at him.

"What's the name of that TV company in Nottingham?" he asked her.

They spent the rest of the day telephoning various people and getting nowhere, being transferred through the TV Company's switchboard to all and sundry, who eventually admitted to knowing absolutely nothing of what they were talking about, or who they were talking about.

They called Martin and told him what had happened. "It was bound to happen some time to my little pest of a little brother, Dad, he headed for trouble wherever he went, it was his life!" said Martin. Then he joined in the hunt for the people in charge of this escapade.

By early evening, they managed to track down the news editor who had sent Gerry out there to collect the story on film, but it was a different story that he was telling now.

"Mr McGuire?" said Jimmy. "My son is wounded in Afghanistan and he and Peter want you to get them back home as quickly as possible."

"Mr Coney," said a cold voice on the other end of the phone, "he knew what he was doing when he went out there, and there's no way I can justify the money to charter a plane to go and get him back. He'll be all right; they deal with wounded soldiers every day. When he can he'll be up and home in no time. Don't worry."

"That's not what his colleague Peter is telling me. They want you to get them home now," shouted Jimmy, getting angrier by the minute.

"I'm sorry, there's really no need to panic, and there's nothing anyone here can do for them at the moment," said McGuire. The phone went dead. After many attempts there was no way of finding McGuire again, his calls had all been blocked.

Jimmy was furious, like Hazel had never seen this quiet man before. It was now 5.30 p.m. They had heard from Peter at 10.00 a.m. that morning. They couldn't call him back and they couldn't get any help. What was there left to do?

Jimmy called the local Army headquarters and tried to get someone to speak to him. Eventually, he got hold of a Commander of some special force who listened to what he had to say. It was no use, the Army couldn't be seen to be going into that area for any reason, just bad politics.

Jimmy slammed the phone down. "My son and his friend are out there and nobody gives a damn! But they will watch his damn pictures on the news without caring about how these pictures got here!" shouted Jimmy. "Why couldn't the bloody idiot be a motor mechanic or a bloody bus driver!"

Martin by this time was also getting short tempered, and then he said that he would have to go home and tell Catherine what was going on, because she would be worrying too.

"Well Dad," said Martin, "the only thing I can see for it, is to fly out there yourself and bring him back, because nobody else seems interested."

Jimmy looked blankly at him for a second.

"You're right, Martin!" said Jimmy, "Ring home and tell Catherine that you're going to take us to the airport."

Martin looked surprised but realising that his father meant what he had just said, he did as he was told.

Jimmy rang the holiday shop where he knew well the man who worked there, as they had booked quite a few holidays and flights from him.

The phone rang. "Is that you, James?" asked Jimmy.

"Hello Mr Coney, how are you, well I hope?"

"James, I need to come and book a flight to Afghanistan right now!"

"What? We are just about to close for the day, and all the computers will start going down soon! Anyway, what's so urgent that it won't wait till tomorrow? Where are you going?"

Jimmy explained quickly all about the emergency and James agreed to wait for him and help as much as he could.

He told Hazel to pack him an overnight bag, along with a few food items and a bottle of whisky poured into an ordinary lemonade bottle. He grabbed his coat and left the house, screaming out of the driveway in the car.

James had already closed the shop but was standing behind the door waiting for Jimmy to arrive.

"We haven't got much time, Mr Coney, the computers could go off at any moment."

"Right. But first, thank you for staying open for me, I am grateful for any help I can get, especially as no one in authority is interested. I need to go to Afghanistan, as near as possible to a place called Kabull, or Kabolt or something sounding like that, and I want to go now."

"You don't ask for much, do you?" said James in a lighter kind of voice.

"Sorry, no time to waste, my son may be killed out there!" replied Jimmy.

"I'm into the programme already after you mentioned Afghanistan on the phone, and this is what is coming up. There's one flight leaving Birmingham at midnight, oh that only goes to Karachi. There's one from Heathrow but that's quite a run from here anyway. Wait, another flight here and there's a connection from Birmingham to Heathrow, and a flight to Kabul, 12.30 tonight! How's that Mr Coney?"

"That's spot on, James lad, get a booking straight away!" said Jimmy, feeling a bit more confident and a little excited.

The computer programme stopped. "Time out" was displayed on the screen.

"What's happening James?" snapped Jimmy.

"The computers have closed down for the evening while all the information is updated ready for business tomorrow," said James.

"What can we do now then?" Jimmy asked desperately.

"Nothing! That's it as far as I can see. Wait!" said James, "I've got another idea. Why don't I phone the airline at Birmingham and see if we can get you a ticket to collect at the desk?"

"Will that work?" asked Jimmy.

"Might do. Sometimes we can do that with ordinary package holidays," replied James as his thin fingers tapped the numbers on the phone.

It seemed like ages, just ringing, until a foreign sounding voice said, "KLM airlines, can I help you?"

James spoke to the woman on the other end: "Yes, have you got any seats left on flight KLM 263 to Afghanistan tonight? It connects at Heathrow at 12.30 tonight."

"Just one moment sir, I'm checking the screen now. No, I think they are all full, it must be some kind of annual festival over there because we've had quite a number of people book seats."

"Please, we've got to get out there, it's an emergency!" said James, prompted by Jimmy in the background.

"Emergency?" the voice came back, "What kind of emergency?"

"My friend's son is out there filming the conflicts and he's been seriously wounded. They're still bombing around the make-shift hospital where he is!"

"Did you say 'filming' out there?"

"Yes, that's right. He's Gerry Coney," said James.

"OH MY GOD!" came the voice over the phone, "Gerry?"

Jimmy grabbed the phone.

"You know my son?" he said.

"Mr Coney, it's Marie, I came to your retirement party with Gerry."

"Marie," said Jimmy, "is there anything you can do. Gerry is wounded and I have to go out there and bring him home. Nobody in authority will help me."

"Where are you calling from, Mr Coney?" said Marie.

Jimmy gave her the shop's number and she said that she would phone back very soon.

Ten minutes went by, it seemed like ten hours. When the phone rang it made both of them jump, and they looked at each other to see who was going to answer it.

Jimmy picked up the phone, "Hello, this is Jimmy Coney, is that Marie?"

"No, it's not. It's Hazel."

"Hazel, what are you doing phoning here, we're waiting for a very important phone call, please, hang up!"

"Ok Jimmy, but just make sure you get two tickets. I'm going with you!" said Hazel and hung up.

"Stupid woman!" snarled Jimmy, "No, I didn't meant that, she's just as worried as me. She's coming too, James, so make it two seats."

"We haven't got any seats yet," said James in a disappointed sort of way. "If this Marie doesn't come up with something soon, the plane will have gone anyway."

Jimmy blew out his breath in exasperation. The phone rang again.

"This is Jimmy Coney, hello."

"Mr Coney, it's Marie."

"What have you got for me?"

"We've just cancelled two tickets because of documentation difficulties, get up here as fast as you can, I've put your name on one."

"Put my name on both of them, my wife wants to come as well," said Jimmy.

"Right, that's done. Come to the desk when you get to the airport, they will be waiting for you."

"Thank you a million, Marie," said Jimmy, "I owe you a dinner when we get back."

He put the phone down and thanked James for his help. "Here mate," said Jimmy, "You've been a great help to me, take this." He pushed a note into James's hand and James protested slightly, then thanked Jimmy.

After he had locked up the shop, he popped his hand into his pocket to pull out the note. It was £50.

Jimmy raced home, collected his bags and Hazel, and Martin whisked them off to the airport. He bought some currency for any little emergency that might come up, and went to the desk, where he was to collect his tickets. Marie came out of the office and handed him a paper wallet containing two air tickets.

"Hazel," said Jimmy "do you remember Marie from the party we had on my retirement? She's been really helpful."

Hazel said hello and thanked her too. She did recall seeing Gerry with a foreign looking girl that night, but it seemed so long ago and much had happened since then. Obviously, their lives had turned completely around from what they used to be. Here they were, jetting off to a foreign country like two spies, at midnight!

"Marie," said Jimmy, "we will never be able to thank you enough."

"I am the air hostess on this flight, and when we land at Kabul I have a forty-eight hour turn-around," said Marie, "so I am coming with you!"

"Blimey, we'll soon have ourselves quite a little army at this rate!" said Jimmy. "And I thought I was going on my own. Any minute now the grandkids will show up and they'll be going too!"

"I know this country, Mr Coney. I have been there many times. And besides being able to speak the language, I am very fond of your son," said Marie.

"Right then, let's get this show on the road," said Jimmy as he marched off towards the checking-in desks.

The plane took off on time and connected at Heathrow as planned. It was full of Asian looking people, some of whom looked as though they were returning to active duty in the terrorist army.

It was a long flight and everyone was tired, but on touchdown in Kabul it was already well into the afternoon and the sun was hot. Marie booked them into a small hotel and told them that she would be back soon to help them find Gerry. Jimmy and Hazel decided to get cleaned up, showered and changed and had a light meal. A couple of hours went by before Marie returned, carrying a map and a set of car keys.

"I have found out where the hospital camp is, but it is very dangerous.

No one is supposed to go out there without military escort," Marie told them. "We are not allowed to hire a car to go there, so I told them we were touring another area and going to the coast."

"By gum lass," said Jimmy, "you've certainly got your head on the right way."

"But if we're going up into the mountains, a little hire car will be of no use whatsoever."

She pointed to the window and Jimmy went over to look out. "Bloody, bloody hell!" said Jimmy who didn't usually swear, "What a load of bloody iron!"

Hazel came over and looked out, to see the biggest four-by-four jeep she had ever seen. "Yes Jimmy Coney!" snapped Hazel, "Since when did you start using swear words like that? All those years with gangs of men and never, ever have I heard you swear!"

"Sorry dear, it just seemed to explain best the sheer astonishment of what I had just seen," said Jimmy.

She hugged him and gave him a little kiss, as if to condone it this time, but no more.

"We should go now before it gets too dark to see much, these roads can be treacherous at the best of times," said Marie. She had changed from her air hostess uniform into what made her look like a regular "commando." Jimmy and Hazel were in jeans and tee shirts, with large sweaters and coats for later.

It looked to be about ten miles up into the mountains to where someone had put a cross on the map that Marie had brought. The journey took some time as it was just a track at times, and when it got wider, it was just a wider track. There was no proper road surface as such; it just changed every time it rained. The countryside was bleak and uninviting, a drab scenery of rocks and trees, with plenty of places for anyone to hide. Not the kind of place for tourists!

Nearer the place there were some lights in the trees to one side, and then a bright light, like a flame, blazed out from the trees some distance away.

"It's a shell!" shouted Jimmy as he swerved the jeep into all kinds of angles to avoid it hitting them. There was a loud bang just behind them and the jeep lunged forward, scraping a large rock along the complete side of the jeep. Another flame shot out from the same place, and Jimmy swerved as the shell exploded with another loud bang just to the side of them. It picked the massive jeep up off the road and they bounced back onto four wheels.

"Everyone ok?" shouted Jimmy.

"Yes, I think so," said Hazel and Marie.

Just to break the tension Marie said to Jimmy, "Perhaps you could drive a little more carefully?"

Laughter broke out and a kind of confidence returned. Some soldiers came out onto the road a little way ahead, and waved their guns, motioning the jeep to stop.

"Blimey," said Jimmy, "we've had it now. What do we do?"

Marie looked hard into the headlight span, and said, "It's alright, these are the Northern Alliance army who will know where the hospital is. Pull in over there and I will go and talk to them."

Jimmy wasn't so sure, but did as she said. Marie got out and shouted something in a different language. They talked to her, with arms and hands making all kinds of gestures, and then she brought one of them back to the jeep.

"Mr Coney, this is Ameir, he will take us to the camp," said Marie as the man climbed in behind Jimmy.

He shoved his big machine gun between the seats and gave Marie some directions, which she interpreted to Jimmy.

There was another flash from behind. The man shouted something in his language. Jimmy didn't wait for the interpretation he just stood on the accelerator and hung on for dear life. People, and the large machine gun, flew all over in the jeep as a big bang went off just behind them.

He directed them to a camp in a clearing in the trees. There was an old Russian tank that had been repaired and was now back in use, a land Rover and an old Japanese army lorry with gun turrets welded onto the roof.

"This is not the hospital!" said Jimmy to Marie.

"No, it is their camp where we will stay tonight. It's not safe to travel after dark," replied Marie.

"You're not bloo... not joking," agreed Jimmy, "after three near misses." And he nearly swore again! Hazel took his eye just in time to pull him up.

They were led to a building and met the commander of the rebel army, who could speak some broken English.

"Welcome, England people," he said. "We take you to hospitalia first daylight, it over hill, but too much danger in night. Make yourself house, rest."

Jimmy got the message, it was 'make yourself at home and get some rest' which didn't sound a bad idea but he didn't realise that these men had to put up with being shelled all night!

The noise and vibration through the ground was horrendous! No one slept at all that night. At daybreak the party set off along some wild terrain, on tracks that had deep holes and ridges in them. After about a mile they came to another clearing in the trees where a makeshift hospital had been erected from anything that could be found. It was quiet and there seemed to be no one about.

"This looks a bit off," whispered Jimmy to Marie. "Shouldn't there be more activity than this for a hospital?"

The man with the big gun got out of the jeep, and cautiously looked around. He said something to Marie and started to look around.

"What did he say?" whispered Jimmy.

"Something is not right, he's worried. There should be many people here. It may be that they have been attacked and have scattered into the woods and rocks."

"Is this where Gerry will be, do you think?"

"Yes, they know of him, they have done lots of filming with him and he is their gateway to the world media."

Jimmy stood there speechless. "Our Gerry? Gateway to the world media?" He all but swore again inside.

Just then some shots rang out in the clearing. Jimmy guessed that the return fire was the man with the big machine gun. Then he felt something cold and steel-like push into his side, and he turned slightly to see the face of a Taliban soldier. He trembled as he looked at Hazel, who also had a soldier with a gun pointing at her. She was rigid. A patrol of Taliban soldiers had found the hospital and battled with the Northern Alliance soldiers, who had gone into hiding. These were the "clearing up" squad, who would wait around to see if any more terrorists appeared.

There was no sign of Marie! She had vanished after the first sound of gunfire.

The soldier said something to Jimmy, but obviously he couldn't understand what.

"English, English!" shouted Jimmy in desperation. The next thing Jimmy heard was the clicking of the hammer of the gun, as it was about to be cranked into action, and take their lives.

All of a sudden the soldier groaned and fell down at the side of Jimmy. Then the other soldier with his gun trained on Hazel, screamed and fell to the ground. Jimmy and Hazel stood rigid and frightened as they watched the first soldier stagger to his feet. As he levelled his gun towards Jimmy and Hazel, they saw a brown boot on a long leg hit him right under the jaw. The soldier fell backwards and stopped moving. Jimmy swung around to see Marie getting up from her flying kick.

Jimmy wanted to swear again, but couldn't speak. Marie grabbed Hazel and hugged her, "It's all right, they will be dealt with in a minute. Are you both all right?"

Jimmy spoke first. "What happened to you, where did you go?"

"I heard the gunfire and went to help. Ameir shot two more of the Taliban soldiers and I saw these two come out of the bushes behind you."

"Hazel, are you all right," asked Jimmy, "you look terrible."

"I'll be all right in a moment. I'm not used to all this excitement."

"Where did you learn all that kind of stuff, then," asked Jimmy.

Marie replied, "My father is Japanese and my mother is English, but we lived in Japan whilst I was growing up, and it was just like an everyday lesson at school."

"We're certainly glad you didn't miss any lessons!" said Jimmy, "and we're very glad that you came along with us, too!"

They heard voices; it was someone calling to Marie in a foreign language. She recognised Ameir's voice and said, "Quickly, he wants some help with something." They ran towards the other end of the compound and found Ameir. He was guiding some people out of the bushes, wounded people from the bombed-out hospital. All three of them helped and got everybody out. Then a familiar voice shouted, "Dad! Mum!" Ameir pulled out the last two people and they were Gerry and Peter.

They all hugged and kissed each other, and Gerry tried to ask, "What on earth are you two doing out here! This isn't the mainstream holiday resort, you know?"

"We've had to come ourselves because we couldn't get any bloody help from any of those bloody boffins back home!" replied Jimmy.

"Dad! You're swearing!" said Gerry.

"Well," replied Jimmy, "they're enough to make a parson swear, that useless lot back home!"

"And I see you managed to bring the one-woman army! How did you know about Marie, to get her to come with you?" said Gerry.

"She was on the ticket desk at the airport," said Jimmy, "and then next minute she was organising the whole trip and everything!"

Gerry told them how Marie had met him when he was working in China some time ago, and helped him out of some hairy situations since.

"I once saw her take out six soldiers with guns, and still had more energy than me to run for our lives," said Peter. "I think Gerry plans his filming escapades around her flight times and turnarounds."

Marie was speaking with some of the rebels and said that it was time they were on their way, as there could be some fierce fighting in a few moments. Some Taliban soldiers had been spotted heading their way, and they would have to find a different road to get back to Kabul.

They piled into the jeep and one of the rebels sat on the bonnet to guide them. Jimmy had to snigger a little, as he had seen the type of roads that they had already come up, and thought that there was no way the rebel would remain seated there for long!

As they set off they could hear the sound of bombing again, and some gunfire. Gerry said to his Mum, "This is a bit different from your car at home?"

"Yes," replied Hazel, hugging her son, "we wouldn't have got far in that. It was Marie who got this for us, she's been a great help." Hazel squeezed Marie's hand in affection, and Marie returned the compliment.

"But do you know, Gerry," continued Hazel, "after all those years on the gas pipes, I've never, ever, heard your Dad swear like he has done in the last few days!"

This brought a bout of laughter ringing through the jeep, and then the rebel bounced up and down on the bonnet as Jimmy hit a rut in the road. The laughter was spontaneous. "Next time you go filming, Gerry, we're all coming with you for the excitement!" shouted Jimmy.

At Kabul airport the plane was ready to leave, and the party only had enough time to have a quick shower, re-dress Gerry's wounds and grab their bags. Marie had already phoned the airline and told them to hold things up for them. They dumped the jeep in the compound for hire vehicles, and it looked like it had been in action in a war rather than on hire to an English couple! It was battered and dented.

It was raining and cold when they landed at Heathrow, but they were not bothered in the least, as they were all back home and safe. While they were waiting for the connecting flight to Birmingham, Hazel rang Martin to arrange for him to pick them up from there. She could only get the main points over to him, as she said, it was all too frightening but exciting!

All four of the weary passengers fitted into Martin's big car and he sped them home. Peter had bid them goodbye at Heathrow, as he lived nearby.

"Well," said Hazel as she opened the front door of their house, "that's been one holiday that I will never forget, although it was only a short one!"

"I think we were lucky to stay alive some of the time," said Jimmy, "especially when those troops caught us in the compound!"

After they had got rid of the baggage and had a cup of tea they said goodbye to Martin, who went home to tell his wife the tales. Then they took Gerry to the emergency department of the local hospital, and dropped Marie off at her house on the way. Hazel smiled as she watched Gerry kiss Marie goodnight; there was definitely something more than colleagues in their friendship, and Hazel was sure that they would see more of her.

At the hospital there was another trauma situation. The doctor called the police when he saw that Gerry had a bullet in his arm, and would not accept the story that they told him. Jimmy was interviewed by the police officers who kept him in a room for nearly an hour before they came out and said, "That's fine, Jimmy, we'll just write out our report and file it. Meanwhile, doctor, get this young man attended to straight away. And thanks Jimmy for the quick response when you repaired our gas pipes that time."

"My pleasure," replied Jimmy.

Hazel was always amazed at how many people knew her husband from the time he'd spent both laying and repairing gas pipes.

Gerry was kept in the hospital for a few days until the wound had healed sufficiently after they had removed the bullet. He kept it as a souvenir, and said that one day he would have it made into a necklace.

Marie visited him when she was in the country, and it was obvious that a relationship was blossoming between them. Hazel had sensed it that night when they took her home, and was now convinced by the regular visits that he received, and the attention.

The story made the headlines of the local newspaper, and after that a national one picked it up too. Apparently, someone in a television company at Nottingham had given them the impression that they were in charge of the whole situation, and that it was they who got him out. When Gerry was told about this his anger got the better of him, and he asked Jimmy to take him to Nottingham. Jimmy couldn't wait for a chance to meet the man, McGuire, face to face. They invited the reporter from the national newspaper to come with them, and he did.

When the three men arrived at the television centre, they were escorted to the office where McGuire was waiting with a champagne reception for them. He didn't know that they had brought a reporter with them, and when the introductions were made, he was not a happy chappie.

"I will not allow a reporter in here!" snapped McGuire.

"Why?" asked Gerry, "Don't you want the truth to be known? How you left it up to my father to buy airline tickets and come out to Afghanistan, with my mother! How you washed your hands of me like Pontius Pilate! You couldn't get me out of there on your budget, no, but you had enough budget to get me out there and screen all my filming on your newscasts!" Gerry was just about at the top of his tolerance level, and the reporter was taking down notes. Jimmy broke into the conversation and asked him whether there would be any money paid out for the rescue mission. "How much do you think it cost us to go out there?" shouted Jimmy, "Not to mention that our lives were in jeopardy all the time we were there!"

McGuire tried to argue that it was not his decision, that there were people above him who had to sanction the spending.

"We will have to have a word with them too!" shouted Jimmy.

"You can't, they won't see you" replied McGuire, "and now if you don't leave I'll be forced to call Security and have you all thrown out!"

"Oh you will, will you," said Gerry, "well we're not going without giving you what we came to give you!" With that, Gerry took a swing at him with his good arm and only caught him lightly on the cheek.

Just as it happened there was a flash from a camera, and the reporter had captured exactly what he wanted. McGuire was about to grin when another fist hit him squarely on the chin, and he disappeared onto the floor behind the desk.

"You deserved that!" shouted Jimmy, holding his hand to try and numb the pain, "We nearly died out there!"

McGuire didn't get up. He was out cold, just as though he had met the left hook of Mohamed Ali. The three men started for the door only to be met by the biggest security man they had ever seen.

"What's going on here, then, where's Mr McGuire?" he said in a tough voice.

"I've just knocked him cold, he's on the floor behind his desk," replied Jimmy, truthful to the last.

The big security man looked over the desk, picked up a sandwich from the buffet that had been laid on, and ate it.

"To think," said the big man, "I would have lost my job if I'd have hit that bastard McGuire, good on you!"

"Can you take us to the people who are above him, the ones who run the budget?" asked Jimmy in a calm voice.

"Why, you gonna do them over as well?" replied the security man.

"No, no," answered Gerry, "we want to try and get McGuire sacked. We were all nearly killed because of him."

"This way," replied the security man, as he grabbed another handful of sandwiches and led them to the lift, and up to a higher office.

"The big man himself!" announced the security guard, "the Director of Current Affairs, Sir Malcolm 'Bastard' Hartley. This is who you need, but don't go in there swinging, please, or he'll send for me. He's a pretty heartless bastard regarding staff, but he'll listen to you lot."

With that the security guard disappeared down the corridor and left them outside a solid wooden door. Not the sort that you would be able to 'kick in' and force entry. Gerry knocked and waited.

"Come," shouted a rather snobbish voice.

With that, Jimmy and his son walked into a very luxurious office. They looked around in amazement before catching the sight of a balding man behind a very large desk. The sort of man who would be ex-service from a very high rank, and it wasn't what he knew but whom he knew.

"Who are you?" demanded Sir Malcolm, "and what are you doing in my office?"

Gerry spoke first, "We came to see that cretin, McGuire, and we've seen him. Now we want to talk to the organ grinder."

"What are you talking about, I'll have you both thrown out of here if you don't leave right now!" shouted Sir Malcolm.

"We're not leaving," interrupted Jimmy, "until we tell you that we were nearly all killed, including my wife, because of your man McGuire, and possibly, because of you!"

"I don't know what you're talking about, but I will listen if you make it short, I have a meeting soon," replied Sir Malcolm in a rather angry voice.

Gerry told him the story of the rescue mission, and Sir Malcolm listened intently when the major names like Afghanistan and Ameir were mentioned. Jimmy interposed on several occasions to get his little bits in. Just as they were about to say "and that's why we're here Sir Malcolm "Bastard" Hartley," the door burst open and McGuire staggered in. The large security man followed just behind him, and nodded to Gerry in a sort of approving manner.

"These men assaulted me!" screamed McGuire, "I want them thrown out immediately!"

"Security," said Sir Malcolm calmly, "show Mr McGuire back to his office and stay with him while he cleans out his desk, then escort him from the premises with the usual formalities, you know, keys, passes, car etc."

"What?" said McGuire.

"You're history!" growled Sir Malcolm, "you're dismissed as of now for misconduct, and we will be checking your budgets tomorrow, so expect a visit from the police."

The security man led him away with, "This way please, Mr Bastard McGuire," closing the door firmly behind them. Jimmy and Gerry looked at each other, then at Sir Malcolm.

"I have watched your career as a freelance journalist for some time, and have noticed that we have used quite a lot of your film in our television news. I am assuming that you were paid handsomely for it?" said Sir Malcolm.

Gerry tossed some figures across the desk, "Handsomely? What do you think, Sir?"

Sir Malcolm glanced quickly at the sheet of paper and shook his head. "We, that is the Television Company, have paid out three times this amount."

Jimmy and Gerry were astonished to say the least.

Sir Malcolm got up from behind his desk, and began to pace around the room. He was very tall and had the look of an ex-guardsman.

Then he said, "Young man, I know that you care very dearly about your colleagues out there in the war zones, and you of all people would not let anything like this happen to them. So, if you agree, and by means of a giant apology I would like you to be the new head of the foreign affairs office, and get me the pictures I want when I want them. Pay these people properly and they will obviously work better for us! What do you say?"

Jimmy nearly answered for him, as this would mean a regular type of job and good prospects, and Gerry would be safe!

Gerry and Jimmy were escorted to the main reception, where Gerry filled out a couple of forms and was given the keys to the car park, office, files etc., oh and a car that was only two weeks old.

"Wait till Martin sees that!" said Jimmy with a big grin across his face.

"It's not all the goodies, Dad, that makes this job right for me, it's knowing that what happened to us will never happen to anyone else, and I will keep a vigilant ..."

Jimmy cut him short, "Get in your new bloody car, dimwit, and don't tell your mother that I swore again."

They laughed with each other and drove off home.

On the way home Jimmy's mobile rang in the car, just outside his house. He quickly got the car into the driveway and answered it.

"Dad," said Gerry, "I'll let you tell Mum what happened and I'll see you in a short while. I'm popping round to see if Marie is home yet."

"All right, son," said Jimmy, "I'll see you when or if you come home later," and went into the house.

"My son has a good job at last!" said Hazel after hearing about their escapade, "Thank God he's finished going out to those horrid countries."

That night there was much rejoicing in the Coney household, and Martin was instantly phoned and given a blow by blow, literally, account of what had happened. Things seemed to be coming right for Jimmy and his family, and he could feel easy in himself that he could now step back from organising everything for them, and let them get on with living their own lives.

That night, as they retired to bed, Jimmy pulled Hazel over to him and gave her a hug.

"What's that for?" asked Hazel, although she didn't mind in the least, "Have you been up to something again?"

"No lass," replied Jimmy in his loving tone, "I just feel really content now that the youngest has got settled at last. He always was a worry, and I know you always worried about him even though you never said."

"Well, you know me," said Hazel, "I can't help but worry and care when he was out in those horrible places, taking pictures of all that atrocious warring."

Jimmy shuddered, "Phew," he said, "it just felt like someone had walked over my grave, is it cold in here to you?"

"It's your age," replied Hazel, "come on, let's get into bed, that'll warm you up."

CHAPTER FOUR

The Last Days

Hazel and Jimmy had just arrived back from a holiday in Majorca, a couple of weeks in the sun after their wedding anniversary holiday in Madeira. As Jimmy put it, "You can't just hang about the house waiting for D. I. Y. jobs to turn up can you?"

The phone rang, it was Martin's wife, Catherine, asking to see if they had a good time and were they sunburnt.

"I've just finished some bacon and eggs, Cath," said Jimmy, "that's the only thing I've missed these last two weeks, because they don't cook them like Hazel does." Cath laughed and told him that they were coming round tonight if they were up to having visitors. She thought they might be tired after travelling, but no, not Jimmy, the man who took on Afghanistan!

"You come round love," said Jimmy, "and bring my two little sweethearts as well, we've got something for them."

"See you about eight o'clock, then," said Cath, and rang off.

Gerry came home at teatime and Jimmy told him that Martin, Catherine and the kids were coming round later.

"Will you be here, Gerry," asked Jimmy, "or are you out tonight?"

"Err no, I'm going to be here, I want to have a word with Big Brother about something I'm planning."

"Oh," said Jimmy, "and what might that be, not some jaunt to another war zone?"

"No," replied Gerry, trying to put him off the scent, "no, it's just a little investment I've seen and I want his advice before I go any further."

"Good thinking, son, you know that he has all that kind of information and he's bound to advise his brother properly, isn't he?" said Jimmy.

"Err yes Dad," said Gerry, "that's right, I'll get together with him when he comes round tonight." With that, Gerry left the room rather quickly and Jimmy was a little bit suspicious.

"Hazel!" he shouted, "Where are you woman? Hazel!" She came downstairs and asked him what all the shouting was about.

"What's Gerry up to, has he told you anything about some investment he's planning?"

"No," said Hazel blankly, "he's said nothing to me Jimmy."

Strange, thought Jimmy, it must be the new job that's having a sobering effect on his spending.

The job at the television centre was going really well, and he was even playing golf with Sir Malcolm by now! He dealt with the news correspondents from all over the world, and sent people to different countries where the news was happening. Jimmy was proud of both his sons, and loved his daughter-in-law Catherine and the two little girls. How contented can a man be, thought Jimmy, and I'm sitting back and enjoying life at fifty nine, well, nearly sixty, next month.

Gerry and Martin had planned a birthday meal at Jimmy's favourite restaurant, and had also included their mother in on the secret. The only person that didn't know was Jimmy.

Marie was on leave, so she was available too, but that was not the only reason for her being asked to the party. Gerry had already proposed to her and she had accepted. Her parents were attending the little gathering as part of the engagement celebration. Her father was Japanese, but had lived in this country for thirty years, and could speak English as well as the next man though you might detect a slight north London accent. Of course, when the plans were finally revealed to Jimmy, Martin took him on one side and said, "Dad, you know that Marie has also invited her parents, don't you? Well, her father is Japanese and doesn't speak much English, so watch how you make any gestures with your hands, just in case he thinks that you're attacking him. We don't want him to kick you in the back and launch you across the room, do we?"

Jimmy looked somewhat surprised, but nodded in agreement, after all, it was Martin saying this. If Gerry had told him the same thing he would have instantly recognised a send up!

The evening arrived, and everyone was washed, brushed up and ready to go. A taxi came for Jimmy and Hazel and they were taken to the restaurant, where they met the rest of the family. Marie's parents hadn't arrived yet, so they all waited at the bar and had a drink.

Each of them had brought a birthday card for Jimmy, and Hazel had secretly brought a card to congratulate Gerry on his engagement, as she knew about it.

Marie's parents arrived. Her father opened the door for her mother in true gentleman style. He was dressed in a black suit and tie, with his black hair combed neatly into a very straight parting. Her mother was wearing a black skirt and a white blouse. She was quite well made but good-looking, and had dyed-blonde hair. Quite a contrast from her husband, although he was very smart and had that oriental look which made him quite handsome. Marie greeted them, giving her mother a kiss on the cheek and her father a kiss and then a gentle bow. He responded with the same, as if they were about to have a few rounds of karate.

"Mr Coney, this is my mother, Linda, mum, Jimmy Coney, Gerry's father."

"Pleased to meet you at last," said Linda, "we've been hearing so much about you."

"All good I hope," said Jimmy with a grin.

"And this is my father, Soichiro Takakura, dad, Jimmy Coney," said Marie.

Jimmy leaned forward and did a sort of bow, shook his hand and said, "Good meeting you, nice daughter," in a kind of broken English as though he would not understand.

Mr Takakura smiled and replied in his north London accent, "Oh ah, she's a good lass really, bit headstrong though at times."

Jimmy's mouth dropped open with surprise, until he heard the roar of laughter from the rest of them. "You sods!" he said, "fancy winding me up like that with a bloke I wanted to give a good impression to."

"No bother, Jimmy," said Marie's father, "and please call me Burt, everybody else does. You know, like Burt Kwouk the actor in the Pink Panther films."

"What you having, Burt?" said Jimmy totally embarrassed, "And don't say a glass of Saki!"

"No fear, mate," said Burt, "I'll have a pint of bitter, please."

"And Linda?" asked Jimmy.

"Oh, a glass of red wine, please, Jimmy."

They were all led to a huge table at the far end of the restaurant and seated themselves around it.

Jimmy led the conversation. "Who taught your girl all those fancy moves then, Burt? She saved our lives in Afghanistan you know."

"Yes she told me all about it," he replied, "I wish I had known that you were going so that I could have come too. After all, (then he said this as though he were speaking broken English) good for student to see master in action too!"

They all laughed.

"Yes, right from being a little girl I have tried to teach her, but it's always difficult teaching your own kids, isn't it?" said Burt. "They seem to take more notice from a stranger than from a parent, so eventually, I sent her to a place to carry on with the lessons."

Jimmy piped up; "Can you do any of them special things then, like breaking a brick ..."

Hazel cut in, "Jimmy! Stop talking so daft, we don't want you to start setting up a competition over the table, so stop it!"

"I just ..."

"No more talk of fighting!" said Hazel. "It brings back those awful memories of that awful place."

Burt saw that Hazel was beginning to get upset, so he quickly changed the subject.

"I'm sorry Hazel, I didn't mean to bring up anything to upset the evening, but I would just like to say, it's a pleasure to be here and see that you all got back safely."

There was a general murmur of appreciation around the table and Burt added, "And what's more, my new friend Jimmy is sixty today! Let's all wish him 'many happy returns and lot's of 'em' mate."

They all responded and glasses chinked as everyone toasted Jimmy.

Off came the jackets and sleeves were rolled up, the men becoming more casual as the evening got under way. The food and wine flowed all evening, and the conversation was free and easy as if they had all known each other for years. Then Gerry tapped a spoon on his glass to draw the attention to his little speech.

"Can I have your attention everybody, please, just for a moment?" The table hushed. "We've all got together this evening and had a great time, and it's good to see my dad enjoying his birthday. What I want to add to that is this, and I hope it makes him, and my mum, as happy as I feel. I know that Mr Takakura already ..."

"The name's Burt!" came a shout from across the table.

"Burt already knows, because I had to ask him first. That is, whether I could marry his daughter, and he said yes."

He looked at Marie and she at him, and then the whole gathering seemed to descend upon them both with hugs, kisses and congratulations.

Jimmy clasped Gerry's hand and while the others looked on, said to him in a very serious voice, "You do know, lad, that the Japanese have a special testing ceremony for would-be husbands for their women?"

Gerry froze as he looked into his dad's face with all uncertainty, and then across at Burt who stared back and nodded in approval at what had been said. Then Jimmy couldn't help but break out into laughter, which set the whole company going too. He hugged his son and wished him 'every happiness'. "I had to get one back on you, Gerry, and I'm sure I'll get that brother of yours before too long," laughed Jimmy.

"You had me going there, dad," said Gerry, "especially with Mr – Burt looking me straight in the eye as well."

"He's one of us, and so is Marie, and we all feel like we've known each other for years," replied Jimmy. Then Hazel produced the congratulations card from her handbag, already written out. She gave it to him and he looked at it. "How the hell did you know about this when I didn't suspect a thing?" asked Jimmy.

"Women's' intuition, dear, that's how," replied Hazel with a wry grin on her face. "The concern when you booked the tickets, all the visits to the hospital; God knows how she managed to fit them in with her flights.

And what about inviting her parents to your birthday party, didn't that tell you anything?"

Jimmy looked stunned, and then kissed her and they handed the card to Marie and Gerry.

"Can't fool your mother," said Jimmy.

A waiter came and announced the arrival of a large taxi for the Coneys, and the evening was over, or so they thought.

"You are coming back to our place, aren't you, for a 'night cap'?" asked Linda.

"Oh, but it's eleven o'clock, it's quite late," replied Hazel.

"No it's not," said Burt, "we only live a mile away from you and we would love you to come round."

"Come on dad," said Gerry, "come and see his Japanese garden."

"Don't start that again!" said Jimmy, and they all laughed.

Apart from Martin and Cath, who had to get back to relieve their babysitter, the rest of them piled into the big six-seater taxi and went to Burt and Linda's. Jimmy was expecting to see a large, palatial dwelling that would make him feel a little bit 'inferior', but instead, their house was more or less just like Jimmy and Hazel's. They seemed to live in the same manner as Jimmy and Hazel too, with all the same wants and ideals. It was as if Jimmy and Hazel were brother and sister to Burt and Linda.

Linda showed Hazel around her newly fitted kitchen, which looked surprisingly like Hazel's. Burt took Jimmy through the lounge and opened the patio doors. He switched on the outside lights that shone over a green lawn with borders infested with weeds and shrubs.

"That's it," said Burt, "the Japanese garden." They both laughed.

"Come on, I'll show you my garage," said Burt with a smile.

"Oh and what's in there then, a karate training gym?" said Jimmy.

"No, nothing like that," said Burt, as he switched on the lights to reveal a nearly new hatchback car, and what looked like a small den in one corner with a table and two chairs. He opened a large fridge and there, stacked on every shelf were bottles and cans of beer, and several bottles of wine. Jimmy couldn't believe it!

"I've been saving this bottle of champagne for a special occasion, and I think that tonight's just that occasion," said Burt.

They went into the house and found half a dozen glasses, which were filled and emptied until all the champagne was gone. Laughing and talking took them into the small hours, and it was time to call for a taxi at three o'clock!

"We'll get together again soon, Burt," said Jimmy as he got into the taxi.

"Don't make it too long," shouted Burt, "we'll be glad to have another good night as soon as you want."

The months flew by and the new friends had many good nights which culminated in a drink at either Jimmy's house or Burt and Linda's. The women went shopping together too, on a regular basis, which meant that Burt and Jimmy didn't have to suffer the job. Gerry and Marie sometimes made it to one of these evenings, when she was in the country. Wedding plans were under way by now, and a date had been fixed to coincide with Marie's birthday, which was six months away. The time went quickly and before anyone knew what was happening, the day had arrived. It was all hustle and bustle as usual on these days, not to mention getting Jimmy to fit into his new suit and shoes.

The car arrived and took Jimmy, Gerry and Martin to the church. Martin was best man and the two little girls were bridesmaids. Hazel had helped Cath to get them ready at Hazel's house, as she had the hard task of getting Jimmy ready as well. The car was returning to collect them next.

There was no talk of "do you think you're doing the right thing?" from anyone, as they were all aware of the closeness between Gerry and Marie. She had the usual offers from pilots and crew, but always in her mind and her heart had been Gerry.

Burt and Linda were rushing around at their house and when the phone rang Linda grabbed it as she passed the table in the hall.

"Hello."

"Hello Linda, it's Hazel. All ready then?" asked Hazel.

"Wish it was!" said Linda, "We're running around here like blue arsed flies and now Burt's lost his cuff links. Oh, he's found them. The car will be here in a minute and Marie is still upstairs faffing with her make-up! I'll tell you what, if we don't make it to the church we'll see you in the pub next door."

"We've been just the same, here. Oh, got to go, the car has arrived for us. See you there Linda and good luck," said Hazel, and she hung up the phone.

Hazel, Cath and the two little bridesmaids got into the car and sped off at a crawl to the church.

Burt, Linda and Marie arrived at about the same time as Hazel, and they couldn't get over the stunning looks of the bride. They were used to seeing her in casual clothes, and sometimes with big boots like a workman, and here she was, the picture of beauty. Hazel hurried inside and found her seat next to Jimmy, and nodded to Gerry with a silent whisper, "She's here."

As the organ played, Gerry turned for a moment to see his beautiful bride, and heard a quiet voice from his dad say, "Blimey, she scrubs up well, doesn't she?" Hazel gave him an elbow in the ribs. Gerry couldn't help turning to his dad and smiling, but his eyes were filling with tears of joy as she came and stood next to him.

Burt looked all the part of the loving father who was giving his daughter away, but he knew that he *was* gaining a son. Everything went according to plan and after the photographs had been taken, it was back to the restaurant where they had announced their engagement for the reception. By now, the manager was more than familiar with the Coney family, and the Takakura family too. Nothing had been too much trouble for this special occasion, although the bill for the meal reflected that of course.

The speeches were concise and meaningful, with no one being short of nice things to say. Gerry was hoping that his dad didn't steal this little bit of limelight for a bash at him, as he always used to call him "dimwit" because of his obsession with going to all those war torn countries. Instead, Jimmy stood up and gave the best speech that anyone could wish to hear.

"My very good friends, dear family members, good neighbours, I have to say that today has been one of the best days of my life. I enjoyed the time when Martin and my lovely daughter-in-law Catherine were married, but I never thought that I would see the day when my son Gerry would finally mature, get a proper job and buy a house, and marry a beautiful young lady like our Marie. (Jimmy always called her "our Marie" because she always seemed like one of the family before they were married) He always seemed to be lost in other people's causes, and filming other people's troubles, without a thought of his own safety or personal happiness. When I look at him now, I can only feel the greatest admiration and joy a father could ever feel, to know that he has finally settled down and got his head on the right way. (There was a general muttering of laughter and Gerry was expecting the time would soon come where his dad would say "dimwit" but so far, the old man was doing all right!) We didn't know Marie until that bother in Afghanistan, and she saved Hazel and me from certain death. Some nights, in my dreams, I can still hear the click of that gun in my side. We are family members with her parents, Burt and Linda, and it feels like we have known *them* all our lives too! I can only say, that I wish this lovely, loving couple all the best of happiness in the world. And who knows, one day they may have a little "dimwit" of their own! A little Gerry, or we can hope for a little Marie, that would be better. (Gerry was laughing, he knew his dad would get that in somewhere, but at least he could only say that word, he couldn't swear as well!) Come on everyone, raise a glass in a toast to the bride and groom! I give you, the bride and groom!"

Everyone toasted, and before they had all sat down, Jimmy fell back onto his seat, clutching his chest.

"What's wrong, Jimmy?" shouted Hazel.

Jimmy looked at her and smiled, "I have a terrific pain in my chest that seems to be moving downwards. I think its trapped wind!"

"Oh, Jimmy Coney," snapped Hazel, "you're so . . . annoying at times. Are you all right or what?"

"It's passing now, it's going off," said Jimmy with some relief.

"What's up Jimmy?" asked Burt and then Linda.

"I just had a sharp pain for a moment, but it must be all the champagne, you know, all the gas in it" replied Jimmy.

"Give us some warning if it's going to come out, Jimmy," said Burt with a grin.

With that, they all started to laugh and Jimmy was back to his normal self again. Burt made a pretend gas mask out of a napkin and put it over his nose and mouth. While it stayed on they all roared with laughter, and when it floated off, that caused a repeat of the laughter.

"I don't know about you, Jimmy," said Burt, "but I reckon I've had enough champagne to sink the *Titanic*, and I'm ready for a real drink, some beer. How about you?"

"Sure," replied Jimmy, "let's get over to the bar for a while, coming ladies?"

"Yes," replied Hazel, "but don't let Gerry and Marie go without saying goodbye, will you?"

"They'll come over before they go, they're not going to run off," said Jimmy.

The bride and groom eventually left for a hotel near the airport, where they would fly to the Maldives the next day, on their honeymoon. Jimmy and Hazel went home in a taxi, as did Burt and Linda. All of them were quite "well-oiled" and a good day had been had by all.

After Jimmy had got himself ready for bed, he sat down on the chair in the corner of the room, where he usually piled all his clothes till the morning. The pain was there again, this time sharper than before. It seemed to go right through his body from his chest to his shoulder blades. He clutched at his chest, just as Hazel was coming into the room.

"What's the matter Jimmy?" shouted Hazel, "Are you all right, I'll ring for the doctor!"

Before she could reach the bedside telephone, Jimmy said in a quiet voice, "Never mind the doctor, get an ambulance, I think this is more serious than trapped wind this time."

As she was finishing the phone call, she saw Jimmy keel over and hit the floor with a bump. All she could do was hold his head and shout to him, hoping to bring him round.

Within minutes an ambulance was at the house, and they tried to revive

Jimmy. His heart started to beat again and they whisked him away on a stretcher, down to the ambulance. Hazel went with them and waited nearby while a team of doctors and nurses worked on her husband. He had stopped breathing and there was no pulse, for the third time. After more attempts to revive him, the doctor in charge looked up at the clock, it was 1.15 a. m. and after speaking to all the other members of the team, they stopped.

While the nurses were clearing everything away, and removing all the pipes and equipment, the doctor came out to Hazel.

"I'm very sorry, Mrs Coney, he had two more heart attacks and the last one was a massive one. His body just couldn't stand it. Was there any history of heart disease with your husband? Has he had any pains or trouble before?" asked the doctor.

"Nothing," replied Hazel, her mind blocked by devastation, "he's never been ill in his life apart from colds or 'flu."

"This always seems quite unfair, to see a fit man taken like this. I have known people with heart trouble live to a ripe old age. It just doesn't seem fair somehow, and you have our deepest sympathy," said the doctor.

"Thank you," said Hazel, "can I see him now?"

"Of course, please come with me, I think they've cleaned everything up now," replied the doctor.

She lay over his lifeless body, and began sobbing tears for her precious Jimmy. Her only love for so many years was gone, taken from her. Then Martin arrived and put his arms around her, crying with her. One of the neighbours who was at the wedding had watched the ambulance arrive and leave, and then phoned Martin. Martin had phoned Gerry at the hotel and told him that something was wrong, so they were on their way home too.

Martin took his mother home after they had said their goodbyes to Jimmy, her beloved husband, and his beloved father. At the house they were greeted by the neighbours, Burt and Linda were there, and Gerry and Marie arrived almost at the same time. When the news was broken to them all, that Jimmy had died, they were all so surprised. They were totally devastated.

The whole night was spent in memories and tears, in an attempt to block out their devastation of Jimmy's death. There was someone missing from the house, from the little gang of friends who had enjoyed so many good times together, it was Jimmy.

There was something missing from the conversation, perhaps a little quip of comedy, it was Jimmy. Hazel had no idea of how she was going to go on living without him being there, but she was given assurances of help and comfort from the boys, and from Burt and Linda.

"We're only down the road, or on the end of the phone if you need us, Hazel," said Linda as they left the house in the small hours of the next morning.

"Thank you, Linda, and you Burt, you're good friends and I feel like you are family as Jimmy said at the wedding," said Hazel.

"We'll come round tomorrow to see if there's anything we can do," said Burt, and they went home.

The two sons went back to their homes, as Hazel said that she didn't want anyone staying with her, she wanted to be on her own and think about their father, in her heart. They understood, and went home, leaving Hazel in the house on her own, with her thoughts.

A week passed before the funeral took place, and there was a large turnout of people who knew Jimmy Coney both from work, and from all the places that he used to go. The pubs, the restaurant, the theatre and even the travel shop where he frequently bargained for cheap holidays. Hazel thought that it was a fine send off, but no matter what was said or done, it wouldn't bring Jimmy back. It was a nice send off for a well-known man.

Arthur James "Jimmy" Coney was dead.

CHAPTER FIVE

Why Me?

It was 1.00 a.m. in the emergency room at the hospital. Jimmy was laid on the bed and the team of doctors and nurses were all around him, doing everything they could to save his life.

Jimmy was unconscious, but during that time he left his body and stood aside, watching what was going on. He couldn't understand at first just what was happening, until he saw himself on the bed. They were pressing down on his chest and trying to revive him. He could feel a strange sensation of pressure on his body.

"I'm out of my body!" he thought. "I must be imagining this! It's like what you read about in those fiction books about people who have strange experiences."

Then he looked through the window in the door and saw Hazel in the corridor, crying and looking very anxious. Martin came, and he started crying too!

"What's up with them?" thought Jimmy, "I'm only . . ."

Then it hit him! I'm on that bed but I'm dying, that's why my spirit is free to roam about! He looked at the team working on the lifeless body of Jimmy Coney, and hoped with all his might, that they would succeed in getting life back into that body. They didn't. At 1.15 a.m. they all stopped, looked at the clock, and began to clear away the pipes and equipment.

"You can't stop now!" shouted Jimmy. "I'm here, get me back! Do something else you bloody morons, I'm here!"

It was no use. No one could hear him.

He floated into the corridor as some doctor opened the door, hoping he could communicate with Hazel or Martin. They couldn't hear him either!

"Hazel, bloody hell fire, Hazel I'm here, look it's me, Jimmy!" he shouted, "Get them back in there!"

He watched as the doctor told her how they had tried and that Jimmy hadn't responded to the treatment.

"I'm not bloody dead, you moron!" shouted Jimmy, "I'm here beside you, you docile cretin!"

But nobody could hear him.

He watched as Martin took Hazel from the bedside, and put her in his car, weeping.

"Martin!" shouted Jimmy, "get them back in there!"

All to no avail, Jimmy watched as they drove away. He floated back into the emergency room and saw the nurses putting his body onto a trolley, wrapped in a black plastic coverall.

"You bloody dimwits!" shouted Jimmy, "I'm here, I'm alive! Where are you taking me?"

He floated along with the trolley to the mortuary, where he watched his body being placed into a stainless steel drawer.

"Bloody hell!" said Jimmy, "I'm bloody dead! But how come I can walk about like this and see what's happening, and why can't these bloody morons hear me?"

Just then, he saw a bright light at the far end of the mortuary, and a man was walking from it toward him. He was a tall, thin man, dressed in black, with a kind face.

"Who the bloody hell are you?" shouted Jimmy in his anger.

"Hello Jimmy, I'm John De'Ath, I've come to take you forward," replied the man in a very soft and kindly voice.

"John De'Ath," replied Jimmy, "you've come to take me forward?"

"Yes," said John De'Ath, "you have to come with me to the next level and be processed. It's all right, you're dead now, and your spirit is wandering about, not knowing what to do next, or where to go from here."

"What to do next? Where to go?" shouted Jimmy. "I'll tell you what I want to do next, I want to get back to my wife and family. I want to go home!"

"Sorry," replied John, "you must realise that you're dead, and now it's time for you to cross over onto the next level of life."

"What the bloody hell are you on about, you psycho, if you were death shouldn't you look like the grim reaper with a big black cape and hood, and a bloody scythe over your shoulder?" shouted Jimmy. By this time he was realising that something was definitely wrong.

"We don't do things like that," replied John in a very comforting voice, "today it's more of a personal approach to bringing people who have died over to the other side. If I *had* appeared to you like you said, with the hood and the scythe, it would have scared the shit out of you, wouldn't it?"

Jimmy nearly laughed at the comic reply, but then realised how serious the situation was. He was DEAD.

"Where do I go from here then, John?" he said politely.

"Come with me, Jimmy, I'll take you to the other side's reception area, where you can meet some old friends and find out what's in store for you," replied John.

"Is this your regular job then?" asked Jimmy.

"You might say so," replied John, "there are thousands of us doing this, twenty four of your hours each of your days."

"Sheesh," replied Jimmy, "is the pay at union rates, too?"

"Now you're getting into the spirit of things, pardon the pun," said John, "you'll be all right, don't worry about anything that you did while you were alive, that will all be taken care of, you'll see."

John took hold of Jimmy's arm and led him towards the mortuary door. As he and Jimmy passed through it they were in another world, and there was another man waiting to greet them.

"I've brought Jimmy Coney to you," said John, and the other man took hold of Jimmy's hand.

"Hello Jimmy," he said, "I'm Andrew, and I'm going to see that you get settled in. I'll answer all your questions and put you at ease regarding your expectations."

Jimmy turned to John, but he had vanished. He looked at Andrew and said, "Who are you then, where's St. Peter and the Pearly Gates?"

"Oh, they're further on, but you must be registered here first," said Andrew, "and then you will be processed and taken to where you should be, or given some work to do before you go there."

"This all sounds a bit too organised for my liking," said Jimmy, "where's all this 'heaven and hell' thing that we were told about in church, then?"

"Yes, I know what you mean, but it's more complicated than that," replied Andrew, "you don't just get into the place called 'heaven' like that, you have to earn that privilege."

"So where is this then?" asked Jimmy.

"This is like the 'reception' as you might say, from where everyone is sent to where they should be, or reassessed and re-directed," replied Andrew.

"So what's going to happen next?" asked Jimmy. "Are you going to let me in or send me to hell fire?"

"Oh please," retorted Andrew, "don't even say that word here, it sends shivers down my spiritual spine to even think of that!"

"How come?" asked Jimmy. "Is it a real place, is it as bad as they make you believe?"

"WORSE!" shouted Andrew, "and don't even say the word again, that's how bad it is!"

"Blimey," whispered Jimmy. Immediately, he couldn't see and shouted to Andrew, "Hey, I can't see! What's going on?"

Andrew touched Jimmy's forehead and he could see again.

"What happened?" shouted Jimmy.

"You must learn to control what you say and think from now on," said Andrew, "you are 'in the spirit' now, and everything has a different way of working. The word that you said is some form of slang on earth for 'God blind me' and when you said it, it happened!"

"Wha ... t?" murmured Jimmy.

"That's right, you now have more control over things than you had in your previous life," explained Andrew, "be careful what you think and say, because that is what will happen!"

"Bloo ..."

"And don't swear, either," Andrew cut in, "that can be really dangerous!"

"I'm not sure that I can handle all this," said Jimmy, "I'm only human!"

"Not anymore you're not," said Andrew, "you're now 'spirit' not 'human' and you will have to learn to live with that!"

"How on earth can I do that?" said Jimmy.

"Simple," replied Andrew, "you will be re-trained to know just what you are now capable of, and when and how to use it. Come, take my hand, I'll take you through the training scheme."

"How long will that take?" asked Jimmy.

Andrew let go of his hand and said, "There, now do you understand more fully?"

Jimmy looked at him, they didn't seem to have moved or been anywhere, yet he knew that his mind was full with a new capacity of supernatural and spiritual things, like he never knew before.

"Wow!" shouted Jimmy, "that was really something!"

"Now you know all things and how to use your spiritual body, let me take you on a whistle stop tour of the place," said Andrew.

"Right," said Jimmy.

"Well, what did you think of that, Jimmy?" asked Andrew.

Jimmy felt like he had never moved an inch, yet could recall all the beautiful sights that he had seen. The lush, green, meadows, trees, warmth, and friends that he hadn't seen for years. They weren't crippled or ill any more, either! There were beautiful valleys, with sparkling rivers like he had never seen before. He dipped his foot into it and felt tremendous, like as if a weight had been lifted from his shoulders! This river had some kind of healing power!

He felt like he had spent two years travelling, yet it was like as if he'd blinked an eye and was back!

"Phew! What's this speed thing, then, Andrew?" asked Jimmy after he got his breath back.

"That's how you travel when you're in the spirit," replied Andrew, "nothing like how you travelled when you were in the 'body' is it?"

"You don't say!" agreed Jimmy, "Speed of light?"

"Faster!" said Andrew with a big grin on his face, "Faster than anything you have ever known! And now that you have been re-trained in your spiritual mind, you know that you only have to think of a place and you're there, think of something that you want and it's there! Think of a person whom you used to know and you can be instantly at their side, though they wouldn't see you!"

"Is that right?" said Jimmy.

"Yes," replied Andrew, "but when you can muster up the right amount of spiritual energy they would probably see you then. Anyway, you're not going anywhere just yet until I've processed you into my computer."

"Computer?" said Jimmy, alarmed to hear that word in the "spirit" world.

"Yes, computer. Where did you think the idea came from on earth?" replied Andrew. "Everything is dealt out to the 'earth plane' as and when they can handle it. We have to let their technology grow slowly, and put ideas into the minds of those that can take it. They are still in their earthly bodies, and some things that we have here would blow their minds if they were told about them too early."

"What about the atom bomb, then?" asked Jimmy, cautiously.

"Oh, I know," said Andrew, disgustedly, " someone thought that it would be a good thing to end that war and then forget about such things, but it all went quite sour with the 'body' people making more of it than we expected. Sometimes, we put part of an idea forward into their minds, and then things have to be left to them to work out, and we just have to sit back and watch what they make of it."

"Don't you get a little bored being here with all this death stuff and spirits?" asked Jimmy.

"Bored?" replied Andrew, "I don't get time to get bored, there's always so much to do. Mind you, sometimes I pop down to a pub and have a quick beer, just for old times sake you know."

"You can do that, too?" asked Jimmy.

"Oh yes," replied Andrew, "you have the ability now to go and do whatever you want, but if you make any mistakes, or transgressions against the spirit world, you are instantly translated back to here for rehab."

"Anyway," said Jimmy, "about Him? Do I get to meet Him?"

"Yes, when you've completed your preliminary stage of rehabilitation. It won't be long," said Andrew.

"What do you mean, type me into the computer?" said Jimmy.

"Oh that was done when I told you about it, there isn't any typing anymore," replied Andrew. "It's all done by telepathy now, no keyboards or screens, just straight into your mind."

"Will that go to earth soon then?" asked Jimmy.

"Some day I suppose we will give them the ability, but how they will use it is another matter," said Andrew with a sigh.

"Probably blow their heads off," agreed Jimmy. "Anyway, Andrew, why am I here when I have done nothing wrong to anybody and tried to live a good life and . . ."

Andrew stopped Jimmy short.

"It's not a question of what you actually did on the earth plane, it's really a matter of time," said Andrew. "Imagine, when you were on earth, and you put fifty litres of petrol in your car thing, when it is all used up the engine would stop, wouldn't it?"

"Yes," agreed Jimmy.

"Well, you wouldn't jump out of it and ask it why, would you? You would automatically assume that it had just run out of petrol," said Andrew.

"Oh, I see," said Jimmy, "so everyone down there has a set time to be there, and then they get sent to here?"

"That's right," said Andrew, "but I wish it was always as easy as that. Sometimes, like you, we have to send someone to get them and direct them straight here."

"What happens if they don't come straight here?" asked Jimmy.

"All sorts of things," said Andrew, "from the haunting of houses and places, to psychic mediums messing about with people trying to relay messages to one another. It causes all sorts of problems when people don't arrive here when they should."

"Can these 'mediums' really get messages through to the people who are still alive?" asked Jimmy with great interest.

"Sometimes," replied Andrew, "depending upon how much spiritual energy the dead person can create in a given moment of earth time."

"That means I could go and see my wife if I wanted, and get a message through via a medium?" asked Jimmy.

"No need for that," said Andrew, "I'm giving you a special job to do for a while to see how you go, to complete your preliminary rehab. I want you to be a spirit guide for those people like yourself, who died before they were old and sick, and don't know where to go next."

"Like that De'ath fellow, you mean?" asked Jimmy.

"Yes, but they're all given that name, all twenty thousand of them," replied Andrew.

"Twenty thousand 'De'aths' going about the world that I used to know as home?" exclaimed Jimmy.

"Oh yes, and that's on a day when I can't spare anyone else. As you know, for a lot of people on the earth plane death is just around the next corner," said Andrew.

"Phew!" gasped Jimmy, "do you know, I never thought of it like that. Anyway, how do I do the job, do I just keep popping down and grabbing someone off the street? I know a lot of people who I'd like to bring here for one reason or another."

"No, no," protested Andrew, "you must obey the call that you will receive from the computer, directly into your head, and then use your own tact and well-known diplomacy to escort them back here. You can use a door or something to make it easier for them, like John did with you in the mortuary. You can be present just before an accident and start to help from there. If you make a mistake or an error of judgement in any way, you will be automatically translated back to me, and I will put you right again."

"You make it sound easy, is it?" asked Jimmy.

"Of course it is," replied Andrew, "you were made for a diplomatic job like this, and it's only for a day, anyway."

"When do you want me to start, and can I see my wife and family?"

"Right now, and yes, anytime you want to see them, just think of one of them and you will be there."

"What if I need food or money?" asked Jimmy, "you know, in the course of looking sort of casual like in a bar?"

"Just put your hand in your pocket, it will be there. Just open your mouth and you will know what to say in every situation. Think of how you want to look, dress, anything, and it will be like that!" replied Andrew.

"Wow, you don't half make it sound exciting, Andy," said Jimmy.

"Well, I wouldn't call it that, but it's what you make of it," said Andrew, "and don't call me Andy! That's what the wife used to call me."

"Sorry mate," said Jimmy.

"You're still here then?" asked Andrew, "didn't you hear my call in your head?"

"No?" replied Jimmy, "Oh, wait a minute, yes! I see what you mean, little bleeping sound, and then, a name and address. Yes I've got it."

"Well get to it then!" said Andrew, "you're on the job now, Mr De'ath!"

"Me, Mr De'ath?" said Jimmy in his mind.

"Yes," came a voice in the back of his mind. It was Andrew, "And don't forget it! While we've been stood about talking, a whole year has gone by on the earth plane and I've processed over one million people so far. Now get to your first appointment, quickly!"

Jimmy thought about the address and was instantly there. It was an old cottage in the Lake District, owned by a middle-aged couple. They had done everything you could imagine to try and make this place their ideal home.

Jimmy looked at his clothes. A plain black suit and black shoes. A black shirt and tie. He pulled a trouser leg up, yep, black socks. This must be the Andrew style, he thought. Then the voice came in the back of his head again, "It is." It was Andrew, who could perceive his every thought. So Jimmy thought to himself, "Andrew, I look like bloody death dressed like this!"

Andrew's voice came again in the back of his head, "You are bloody death, moron!"

Jimmy was quite shocked at the reply, but then realised that Andrew was having a laugh with him, in his corny kind of way.

So Jimmy had another thought for Andrew's open mind ears, "Andy baby, you're gonna have to cut me some slack if you want this mamma to get you these souls, man!"

There was no reply for a second or two, then Andrew came back in. "Jimmy, you're gonna do all right in this job, just use your common sense and your sense of humour. Signing off now, good buddy, this is a ten four and out from the heavenly babe to my man in the scan."

Jimmy laughed to himself, and realised that Andrew did have a sense of humour, and had just switched off for the time being, until he really needed to contact Jimmy again.

Jimmy looked again at the suit and the black shoes. "Nah," he thought, "let's get smartened up, Jimmy lad. You never dressed like this in your life, so no way am I going to look like this when I'm dead! His words rang into his mind – I'm DEAD! And I'm laughing and happy! But I'm dead and I shouldn't be happy! What's Hazel doing? She'll be upset and crying! And here's me having a joke with another DEAD bloke!"

Andrew came in again, "Jimmy, you're dead and you won't ever come back to life, this is it for you lad, now get on with your new life!"

"Sorry, Andrew," replied Jimmy, in his thoughts, "I guess it's just hit me, what's happened and all that!"

"Get this job done quickly and you can go and see Hazel and the family if you want, before I give you another assignment," said Andrew.

"Thanks mate," thought Jimmy, "you're an angel, do you know that?"

Jimmy just thought of what he had said, of course Andrew is some kind of angel, he's in heaven!

Right! thought Jimmy. Best suit from Saville Row, smart brown shoes and socks. No! Brown boots with a zip up one side. Always fancied some of them, but Hazel always said I had to have proper shoes. Flowered tie and ... blue shirt! That's it, now how do you look, handsome? He thought of a long mirror in front of him, and it appeared to be there. Then he made it go away and started towards the house. He didn't have to knock, he just walked straight through it, with a little laugh.

Inside the house was one of the nicest couples you could wish to meet.

He was busy doing a project with the light in the centre of the room ceiling, while the 'missus' was standing below dishing out instructions and safety tips. You know the kind of situation, she knows how to do it properly but gets him to do the actual work. And he doesn't need the nagging!

Jimmy stood watching, after having a look around the room. "Hmm, nice picture of a country scene," he thought. Then as he turned to go into the kitchen, the phone rang and the woman went into the hall to answer it. While she was gone, the man fell off the chair and landed on his back, hitting his head rather hard on the concrete floor. It knocked the stuffing out of him! Jimmy went over in a natural attempt to help him, but realised, he couldn't. As he approached, the man got up and saw Jimmy coming to his aid.

"It's all right mate," the man said, "I think I've just twisted my neck a bit, it hurts!"

Jimmy looked at him and said, "You've done more than that pal, and it's had a real nasty effect on you, that little fall off the chair!"

The man looked at him. "Anyway, who the hell are you, and what are you doing in my house?"

Jimmy opened his mouth and out came, "I'm James De'ath, and I've come to take you across to the other side." Jimmy heard himself say that, but it wasn't what he was going to say.

"The other side?" enquired the man, "what other side of what?"

Jimmy looked kindly at him. "You've had a nasty fall. Look, your body is still on the floor, and I'm talking with your spirit."

The man looked at the body on the floor. He looked at Jimmy. "You're death?"

"Yes," replied Jimmy, "but we don't have the black hood and the scythe anymore because it puts people off."

"Where are you taking me, did you say, across the other side?" asked the man again.

"Yes," replied Jimmy, "and I'd like you to come with me right now. There's no use waiting for your wife to come off the phone and find you, because by that time, there will be no chance of bringing you back to life anyway. And there are many of your old friends and relatives who will be waiting to see you."

"After living with her for thirty years, I'm ready right away, mate, let's go!" said the man.

Jimmy took him to the door in the far side of the room, and although it was the closet, as he opened it and stepped through, there was Andrew.

"Well done, Jimmy," said Andrew, "you can go now and see your family. I'll be in touch."

Jimmy thought of Hazel and was immediately where she was, at his graveside in the cemetery, putting on some fresh flowers.

"Jimmy, my darling," she said to the writing on the stone, "you know I always loved you and thought the world of you. Why it had to be like this I'll never know. I just know that I miss you loads, and would love to see you again, even if it were only to tell you that I love you. I've tried going to the church down the road but it's no help, they don't understand. I can't talk to the family because it only upsets them all if they think that I haven't got over it yet. I'll never get used to not having you, Jimmy. I got all the insurance monies and the pension, but it still won't bring you back, my love."

Jimmy felt tears rolling down his cheeks, but how come? This shouldn't happen to a spirit should it?

Andrew's voice came in his head, "Not usually Jimmy, but I allowed you this just to help you get over it a bit better. If you want to make her feel your presence, gently blow your breath over her, and she will know it's you. This will comfort her, believe me."

"Thanks Andrew, you're a real mate," thought Jimmy, back to him.

He leant over to where Hazel was kneeling and gently blew a breath of air over the side of her face. Then he stood back and waited for the result.

Tears began to roll down her cheeks and a great big smile came upon her face. She stood up and turned a slow circle shouting at the top of her voice, "Jimmy Coney, I love you, I love you!" Then she packed up her bag of dead flowers and rushed towards the gate, dropping her rubbish in the bin as she passed.

Jimmy watched as she practically ran down the street, caught a bus and went home. He joined her at home, to see her pick up the phone and call Marie.

"Marie?" she said, "I'm glad I caught you in, I've got to tell someone what happened to me in the cemetery today."

Marie listened to the story and shared her joy, believing every word. If she had called Cath or Martin, they would have been more concerned that it seemed like she wasn't getting over it, and needed professional help!

Marie told Gerry, and her father. They were happy for her, and if it helped, so what if it was all in her imagination.

Hazel knew what she had felt. She knew that was Jimmy telling her that he was all right!

Jimmy looked around the house. It was still exactly the same. Nothing changed or moved. He looked around the garden and it was the same. Hazel had allowed nothing to be touched, and it was still just as Jimmy had left it.

He stayed a while and watched as she busied herself in the kitchen and made a cup of tea. All the time there was this big smile on her face, and he sensed happiness in her heart. It comforted Jimmy to know that she was all right, and it comforted Hazel to feel that Jimmy was all right and near to her.

"Andrew," thought Jimmy, "can I make myself appear to her, just for a moment?"

"No, not yet," came the reply, "you will probably scare her to death dressed like that."

Jimmy smiled to himself, and left through the front door, without opening it of course!

I want her to see me and to tell her everything is all right, and most of all, I want to hold her like I used to, thought Jimmy.

"In a while," came Andrew's voice again, "very soon Jimmy."

"What! She's not going to die is she?" asked Jimmy.

"No, but I've been given special permission for my new agent to make sure he's sorted, ok?"

"Next job then, Andrew," said Jimmy, and he received another name and location.

CHAPTER SIX

Secret Lemonade Drinker

Jimmy's first day had passed quite quickly, really. He had brought across to the other side some seventy people and was heading back to Andrew for further instructions. When he arrived at Andrew's usual place, he wasn't there. Jimmy thought hard about Andrew and was immediately translated to a pub in the north end of London! Strange, thought Jimmy, why have I arrived here? A quick look along the bar gave him the answer. There, on a stool at the far end, was Andrew, drinking a pint of dark beer.

Jimmy had to have a go with this one, so he changed himself into jeans and a sweatshirt, trainers and long black hair to his shoulders.

As he approached Andrew, he could see that Andrew was sensing a spirit's presence, but couldn't quite pick out who it was. Jimmy got onto the stool beside him and ordered a pint of bitter, and looking round to Andrew said in an Irish accent, "Can I get you one too, me ol' cocker? I don't want to drink on my own, to be sure, do I?"

It was the worst Irish accent that Andrew had ever heard, and he laughed as Jimmy changed back into the suit and blue shirt.

"You had me going then!" said Andrew, his face beaming with laughter and delight, "I didn't recognise you at first."

"Hey, Andrew, how do you drink this if we're spirits, and how do we taste the taste of it?" asked Jimmy.

"You must create a thought that directs your energies into producing what looks like a body, then you can be seen and move about the earth plane and people think that you're just another person. Actually, you might be better doing your job that way, I will change your status … There you go, now you can be like a human body, but you can still walk through walls!" Andrew and Jimmy laughed.

"Does this mean that if I go to Hazel she will be able to see me?" asked Jimmy cautiously.

"See you, and touch you!" replied Andrew, getting a little worse for the drink.

"How much of that stuff have you had, Andrew?" enquired Jimmy, like an overbearing big brother.

"I think this is ten, but I come here once a year on my birthday," laughed Andrew.

"What … no I daren't ask," said Jimmy.

"No need to, matey," slurred Andrew, "I can read you like a book! Eh eh, eh eh. Of course I don't go to the toilet, because I'm a spirit, aren't I? All I do is decide that I have had enough, and will it to go back into the barrel. It's even purer for going into my mouth than it was when he served it to me! Even the money goes out of his till, and doesn't know anything, or anything, or … oh, what's the bloody word? Doesn't know I've been!"

"Andrew, don't you think it's time you got back to the office," said Jimmy, "someone might be looking for you?"

"They will know where I am, silly bugger, I am a spirit!" slurred Andrew. "But, perhaps you're right, I'd better be off."

With that the bar tender came across, and said to Jimmy.

"Is he with you? I think he's had more than enough, get him out of 'ere before he brings it back all over the floor."

Jimmy nodded and proceeded to help Andrew off his stool. When his feet touched the floor he looked up, and then straight at Jimmy, and then said in a cool, sober voice, "See, Jimmy, sober as judge. It's all gone back into the barrel by now, in the twinkling of an eye."

Jimmy was amazed to say the least. Then he remembered that he'd had a pint of lovely bitter, and paid for it! He thought for a second and the beer had gone from his body back into the barrel.

"This is all right, Andrew," said Jimmy, "I can use this as a means to contact the souls that I am taking over to you, and look like just another person."

"Yes," replied Andrew, "it could prove quite a useful tool for you."

"Anyway," said Jimmy, "my day of working is over, in fact, I've been doing this job for twenty FIVE hours now," said Jimmy.

"Seconds of time," said Andrew.

"What do you mean," asked Jimmy, "seconds of time, I'm saying hours!"

"Didn't you ever read in the Bible where it says, 'A thousand years on earth is like a day in heaven?'" replied Andrew.

"No?" answered Jimmy, "you're not telling me that I'll be doing this job for a thousand earth years are you?"

"Just one day my friend, that's all I asked of you and you said yes," replied Andrew.

"But I didn't know how long a day was, then, did I? Anyway, I like doing the job and I like being friends with you," said Jimmy.

He and Andrew shook hands, and Andrew decided it was time to go back. "See you in a second or two, Jimmy?" He laughed a little and Jimmy saw the joke, "Oh, and thanks for a nice birthday, too." He walked out of the pub doorway and vanished into thin air. Jimmy had a little smirk on his face, and then did the same, only he went to where Hazel was at that time. Now he had to remember that he could be seen, or not seen if he didn't want to be. He thought for a while. Hey, that Andrew shares the same birthday as me! It's my birthday today as well! He made himself spirit again and walked through the wall and into the living room. On the mantle piece above the fire was a picture of Jimmy with Hazel, and a candle was burning at each side of it. Apparently, someone had told Hazel that this would encourage his spirit to be at ease if he came back to the house. A neighbour had been going to a medium for some time and some of the things that she was told, she told to Hazel. Hazel would not go with her, as she didn't believe in all that mumbo-jumbo. But she lit the candles, and it looked nice. It made *her* feel better.

She came into the room and looked at the picture. "My Jimmy, you'd have been sixty one now if you were still alive. How I miss you my darling, and how I wish I could just hold you for one more time."

An idea came into Jimmy's mind: If I could approach her in a soft and subtle manner, then appear, it won't frighten her so much.

Andrew's clear voice sounded in his mind. "When I visited my wife, I blew out the two candles, one at a time, very softly. Then I made my voice come through, and then when I thought she was ready I appeared to her."

"Did it work?" thought Jimmy.

"Yes," came back the reply, "and you can do the thing with your body now, but speak softly to her first."

"All right, Andrew," thought Jimmy, "I'll give it a go."

Jimmy waited until Hazel had dried her eyes a little, and then like a soft and gentle breeze, he blew one of the candles out. Hazel looked, and then looked around to see if someone had come into the house, and the draught had blown it out. Then she saw the second one go out and felt that breath that she had felt in the cemetery that day.

"Jimmy, you're here aren't you?" said Hazel with a smile on her face, "Jimmy, I'm not frightened of you my darling, I love you."

Jimmy, frightened that he might frighten Hazel, tried a few words. Softly he said to her, "Hazel. Hazel I love you."

The sounds echoed around the room and Hazel started to cry with joy, not fright!

"Jimmy," she shouted, "come home to me if you can."

Jimmy decided to do it as gently as he could. Andrew's voice came again, "Go over to the curtains, make them move a little to focus her attention. She will then be expecting you to appear. Then get into your body mode and appear."

"Thanks, Andrew," thought Jimmy, and did just that. First though, he dressed himself in the suit that they had put on him when he was laid in his coffin, as she would recognise that. It was his best going out suit, and that's what he went out in, in his coffin. He ruffled the curtains and watched as Hazel, with an excited and expectant look on her face, waited for something to happen. It did! Jimmy appeared to her.

"Hazel, don't be afraid, it's me, Jimmy," he said.

"I'm not afraid my darling, I'm so happy," she replied, gripping her hands as if to try and wake herself from a dream.

"I want to hold you, like I used to," said Jimmy, his soft words echoing like whispers around the room.

Hazel approached him slowly and held out her arms, without a trace of fear, after all, this was her dearest wish come true.

Just then, the back door opened and the neighbour who always went to the medium came into the living room, shouting Hazel's name.

Jimmy switched off from body mode to spirit mode and made himself invisible again. But he had to stay to hear the result of his visit. Hazel stood transfixed for a moment, and then a look of disappointment came across her face.

"Hazel," said the neighbour, "I was wondering if you would like to come with me tonight to David Good's, you never know, you might get a message from Jimmy!"

Hazel was still a bit dazed. Had she seen Jimmy? Would she have been able to touch him? She might never know if that interfering neighbour hadn't opened the back door right at that moment.

"Yes, I'll come with you Margaret, tonight, and I hope that Jimmy will come too!" said Hazel, almost as if to invite Jimmy along, that is, if he could hear her.

"I think I might just pay David Good a visit tonight, and see if he is in touch like he claims to be," thought Jimmy. Immediately he was translated to Andrew's side.

"Done something wrong, mate?" asked Jimmy.

"No, not really Jimmy, but I wanted to have a word with you about visiting a medium," replied Andrew. "It's not usually a 'Good' idea, pardon the pun, but actually, he's your next contact and it will be tonight. You will find him to be a fake, and after you have had a bit of fun with him and his 'séance' you can bring him over."

"I think I'm going to enjoy this, Andrew," said Jimmy, smiling, "I know just how I'm going to play it too!"

"Well, it does seem a 'Good' plan, Jimmy, pardon the pun," replied Andrew, who of course, had just heard what Jimmy was planning in Jimmy's mind, "but take it carefully with Hazel, won't you?"

"You betcha," replied Jimmy, "anyway, I want a word with you!"

"What?" asked Andrew with a smile, as if he didn't know what was coming next.

"How come you like beer so much, and you can slope off to the pub whenever you like?" asked Jimmy.

Andrew found the time to explain all this to his eager friend, who listened intently.

"When I was a man on the earth plane some six hundred years ago, I was the landlord of my own little pub."

"You've been here for six hundred years?" said Jimmy, shocked!

"Yes, but don't interrupt," replied Andrew and carried on with his life story.

Andrew's Life:

"When I was a man, alive and living on earth, I was the landlord of my own little pub. I brewed a lot of my own beer and wines, and bought some from passing traders and monks. It was fourteen hundred and something, the year, and my pub was the best in the district. It stood just inside Sherwood Forest near Nottingham, and it was called The Blue Boar Inn. I suppose that you could say that nearly half my regular customers were outlaws, but everyone was poor in those days. I remember Robin Hood coming in quite regularly, and he used to hold little meetings there, in a certain corner of the inn. We also had regular raids from the sheriff and his men, and some very bitter battles were fought where lots of soldiers and outlaws were killed.

"One day in particular, when the sheriff and his army came, Robin Hood and his men fought them all off. The next day, the sheriff returned with as many men again, and threatened my family and myself. Of course, I denied any knowledge of who came to my inn, they were just customers to me. But that wasn't enough for that wicked man; he took out his sword and plunged it through the body of my daughter. She was eighteen years old, and died instantly. I screamed at him and begged him to leave us alone, and he did, after he had sliced off my wife's head with the same sword.

"Some friends had heard the noise and came to see what was going on. It made them ill to see what had happened. After a while, some outlaws came and helped me to clear everything up, and bury my family at the back of the inn. The next few days I stayed in my bed, sobbing for my family. About a week later I was downstairs trying to get back to normal and earn a living, when the sheriff and his men arrived. Robin Hood and his men were at the inn and the fiercest of battles was fought, right outside my door.

"The two serving girls and myself hid in a back room till it went quiet. Then the door was flung open and there stood the sheriff, blood all over him, and a face like thunder. He pulled one of the girls to him, held her and asked me where he could find the outlaws. I screamed at him that I didn't know. He stabbed her to death with a fancy handled dagger. As she fell to the floor, he grabbed hold of my arm and pulled me over to his side. I couldn't tell him anything; I didn't go into the forest, ever! The last thing I remember was the feel of his dagger's blade across my throat and I collapsed in a heap on the floor.

"Of course, my spirit got up and met someone like you who brought me across, and I've been here ever since! I hadn't been here very long when I watched my predecessor send the spirit of the sheriff and some of his men to the other side!

"But I can't hold a grudge, it was just a case of being there at the time when my time was finished. He may have been instrumental, but it was all meant to be. He was given plenty of opportunities to repent of his wrong doings, but he never took them. He was pure evil! My wife and daughter are here and sometimes I still meet them even though up here there's no real 'belonging' to each other any more, but you do know who people are and what they meant to you on earth."

"Wow!" exclaimed Jimmy, "I would never have thought that I would meet someone who I probably thought was just a character from a legend! You actually knew Robin Hood?" asked Jimmy.

"Oh yes," replied Andrew, calmly, with a strange grin on his face, "he's in another section right now, but when you've got time I'll take you to meet my brother, Robin."

"Brother …" Jimmy was struggling to take this in when Andrew cut him short.

"Shouldn't you be visiting the séance about now, Jimmy?" asked

Andrew, beaming with delight.

"The séance!" shouted Jimmy, "I must have missed it by now, Andrew, and that's with you talking!"

"It's all right, Jimmy," replied Andrew, "you're not tied to time any more, haven't you realised that yet? Just think yourself to be anywhere you want, at any time you want, even thirty years ago if you want. This is like I told you and like you were trained, you are now spirit so get on with life, pardon the pun."

Jimmy remembered some part of his training that sounded more like a chapter from H G Well's book, *The Time Machine* and thought carefully about where he should be and what time it should be. He vanished from Andrew's place and was immediately outside an old house near to where he used to live.

"This is the house of the medium, David Good, fake, taking money from old ladies," thought Jimmy, "smokes like a chimney and takes drugs too! That can't be very good for you, can it?"

CHAPTER SEVEN

Save the Last Séance For Me

Jimmy stood outside the house for a moment as a car pulled up at the kerb. He recognised it as his, or rather, Hazel's now. From the front passenger door emerged the figure of their next-door neighbour, Margaret, and then from the driver's door Hazel got out. Now, how was he going to get to be near Hazel, without frightening her or being too obvious around the table? The front door of the house opened and a woman, dressed all in black, like the owner of a funeral parlour, greeted them. "Goodness me," thought Jimmy, "this really looks the business, doesn't it?"

"That's one of the reasons why you're here," said Andrew's voice, "go on in and get the job done."

Jimmy walked through the wall and into a dimly lit room. The usual thing, a large round table with a large shaded lamp shining into the centre of it, and a large winged chair on one side. The lamp only lit enough of the room to let you see the table and who was sitting around it, the rest of the room remaining dark so as to cloak the secret goings on. All the chairs except one were occupied, and that was next to Hazel. Jimmy walked over to where she was sitting, adopted the 'body' mode, and sat down beside her. At first she didn't look to see who had sat down beside her, until Jimmy put his hand on her shoulder. Then she turned, and even in the dim light recognised her dearly departed husband. She held his hand and tears flowed gently down her cheeks. Then he kissed her on the cheek and reassured her, "Don't be afraid, it's really me."

She whispered back, "I'm not afraid Jimmy, I'm so happy. I would come back with you wherever it is that you've come from if I could."

"It's not your time yet, lass," answered Jimmy as quietly as Hazel was speaking, "but one day I'll come and fetch you. Till then, I have to take people there who are lost or who are unsure of what to do when they have died, that's my new job."

"I'm so proud of you, my Jimmy Coney," answered Hazel. As far as she was concerned the séance was finished as she had got what she came for.

"This David Good is a fake, did you know?" asked Jimmy.

"I never believed in all this stuff anyway, Jimmy, I only came in the hope that you would come to me," replied Hazel.

"I've come to take him back with me, tonight," said Jimmy, "this is his last performance and you are going to have such a 'Good' time tonight, pardon the pun. I must have picked that phrase up from somewhere, I keep saying it and I never used to."

Hazel smiled, and then the door opened and in strode the medium, David Good. He sat himself down in the big chair and looked serenely around the table, just like King Arthur and his knights. He wore a black suit and had a black cape around his shoulders, just like an actor. He welcomed everyone and explained a few of the house rules, who could talk, who should talk, when to ask questions and when not to. He also explained his credentials and experience of the 'spirit world' and 'spirit guides' and the whole of the meaning of life and death as he saw it. What he didn't tell them was that this was all a giant scam to release the feelings of sadness and the contents of the wallets from his audience.

If he had been genuine, he would have sensed the presence of a spirit sitting across the table from him, but he didn't of course.

The lights were dimmed, and the séance began. At first, the medium made himself go into a trance, which was quite easy for him as he had just snorted something up his nose before he came into the room. Jimmy watched and waited as he curdled some words with his head bowed down, and then looked straight ahead with his eyes wide open.

"There's someone coming through," he said, "it's a man and he's looking for Emily, Emily, is there an Emily with us?"

A woman beckoned and then quietly said, "I'm Emily, is it Eric?"

"Yes, that's right," replied David Good, "it's your Eric, he wants to tell you that he's all right and thinks about you all the time."

Emily began to cry a little, and the person beside her tried to console her. Jimmy looked around and saw, in the darkness, someone standing in the corner of the room. This was Good's assistant who would be providing the evidence of a spirit's presence.

As Good continued, he announced that there was someone coming through calling for Margaret. Margaret had come with Hazel and she immediately nodded and said that she was Margaret. Good then began to tell her that her husband was here and that he wanted to make sure that she was all right. Margaret nodded.

"Is there anything that you want to ask him?" said Good.

"Yes," replied Margaret confidently, as she had been here many times, "is he still having any trouble with his heart?"

Jimmy nearly fell of the chair whilst trying to control his laughter inside. "They don't honestly believe in all this, do they?" he asked Hazel.

She quietly 'shushed' him.

Good was telling Margaret how her husband didn't have any trouble with his heart any more, and that he wanted to say that he was enjoying the place where he was. The assistant moved into a position where he could gently brush the shoulders of Margaret, which made her think that her husband was really in the room.

Jimmy could hardly contain himself, but he only had to wait another few moments before it was Hazel's turn to meet her departed husband.

"Now I have a voice coming through to me, it's asking for Hazel, Hazel, Hazel and there is a 'C' for the next part of the name. Do we have anyone called Hazel with us tonight?" said Good in his spiritual wailing voice.

Jimmy saw the assistant move close to Hazel's side, ready for the 'brush' tactic, so he began to speak in his whispering spirit voice. As he did so, he lifted the table up slightly and let it drop with a bang!

"Hazel ... Hazel Coney," whispered Jimmy.

Good opened his eyes with a startled amazement on his face. He wondered who was doing the spirit voice thing and moving the table, after all, it wasn't him!

"I have come to speak with my wife Hazel, and to tell her where the insurance policies are. These will make you very rich my darling," whispered Jimmy. The voice echoed around the room and sounded more "spooky" than Good's wailing voice.

Jimmy lifted the table again, this time high enough to make everyone have to stretch to keep their hands on it. Then it banged down on the floor again.

Good couldn't believe his ears or his eyes, a rich person around his table, he could milk her dry! But wait, he thought, it's not me doing the voice! He looked around the table but couldn't see anyone talking.

The assistant thought that this was Good doing the voice and moved towards Hazel.

Jimmy moved his chair, which hit the assistant on the knee, very hard. Everyone heard the sound of somebody stumbling in the darkness, and they began looking around to see what was happening. Good was annoyed to say the least, and tried to regain the attention of his audience.

"Please concentrate!" he shouted, "the spirits will go away if we don't all concentrate, please!"

The people around the table looked back at their host and the séance continued. Good tried to continue with the visitation for Hazel Coney, he had to establish those insurance policies.

"Who am I talking with?" wailed Good.

"I am Jimmy, Hazel's husband," replied Jimmy in that whispering voice that filled the whole room. Good looked around the table again and saw Jimmy sat beside Hazel, holding her hand.

By this time, the hair on the back of everyone's necks was standing on end, they had never heard Good be this "good" before!

"Jimmy," wailed Good, "come and establish contact with your loving wife, she needs to feel your presence."

Jimmy saw the assistant moving towards Hazel's chair, limping slightly, so he took a breath and began to blow gently towards him. Then he blew harder and a little harder, until the assistant was really leaning forward into the strong wind. Then Jimmy stopped blowing, and the assistant flew forward and fell across the table. Everyone was startled and wanted to know what was happening, and who this man was that was dressed in black, who had just fallen across the table from nowhere. Jimmy tilted the huge table and the assistant slid across its highly polished surface and into the lap of David Good.

The séance broke up, and people began to leave, murmuring about the goings on in the dark. Margaret sat still, waiting for Hazel to move, but she stayed in her chair. Good was about to storm out of the room until Jimmy flicked on the lights from where he was sitting.

Good stopped in his tracks. "Who are you!" he snapped, as he came over to Hazel and Jimmy, "You are responsible for ruining my séance tonight, aren't you? It was you doing that voice, wasn't it? How did you move this table?"

Hazel said nothing.

Jimmy stood up and looked at Good. "You are a bloody fake, David Good, and it's not as if you're any good at it too. It has been noticed in the upper circles," said Jimmy, casting his eyes towards the ceiling and then back at Good, "you have been very naughty, not to mention the abuse that you have caused to your body. That's why I've been sent to take you across to the other side, where you reckon to have been talking to spirits, tonight!"

Good looked like a scared rabbit in the headlights of an on-coming car.

"You, you, mean I'm going to die, tonight!" spluttered Good.

"That's right," replied Jimmy, "right now in fact, if you're ready."

"Who do you think you're kidding, matey?" snorted Good. "You really had me going then for a while, but I know what your game is! You're trying to frighten me off, aren't you, and then you think you can move in on my clients! Well, it won't work! I'll call the police and have you ... thrown out!"

"Hazel," said Jimmy, "call for an ambulance to come to this address, right away."

Good was scared, and he fled into another room and locked the door. When he turned around, he saw Jimmy sitting on a chair by the fireside.

"How did you do that?" he ranted, "Who are you, anyway?"

"I'm James De'Ath and I've come for you, David Good," replied Jimmy calmly.

Good unlocked the door and ran out of the room, down the passage and into a back room. He pulled the stout bolts across the door and wedged a chair under the handle.

"That should keep the paramedics out for a while," said Jimmy.

Good spun round and saw Jimmy standing behind him, arms folded like a disapproving schoolteacher.

"Who the bloody hell are you, you maniac, and why don't you leave me alone?" screamed Good.

"I can't leave without you, David," replied Jimmy, "it's your time to go across, so why don't you unlock the door and make it easier for those who are coming to try and save you?" Jimmy made the chair float away from the door, and then shot the bolts back with a loud bang.

Good tried one more attempt to rid himself of Jimmy, by trying to get through the door quickly. Before he could go any further, he clutched his chest and fell onto the floor. Jimmy waited for a few seconds, and he could hear the approaching footsteps of the paramedics coming down the hall.

Good's spirit stood up beside him, and looked at Jimmy. "They'll save me won't they?" asked Good in a frightened voice.

"Afraid not, mate," replied Jimmy, "they will try but to no avail, because you're coming with me."

With that, he took hold of Good's arm and led him through a door on the other side of the room, to where Andrew was waiting.

"Ah, Mr Good," announced Andrew, "we've been waiting for you. You're quite famous in our circles, did you know?"

"Famous," answered Good, "how do you mean famous? And where am I?"

"We've been monitoring you for some time," replied Andrew, "both with the seances and your ordinary life of abuse to your body! Of course, it was only a matter of time before you finally came across to the spirit world, the world that you so often entered with your fee-paying clients."

"I never meant them any harm!" retorted Good in his defence.

"You never did them any good either," replied Andrew, "pardon the pun!"

CHAPTER EIGHT

Who You Gonna Call? – Ghost Buster!

Jimmy was up at Andrew's place waiting for his next client, when he noticed that Andrew was receiving some sort of communication from somewhere.

"What's happening, Andrew?" he asked.

"It's the boss, he's telling me of a situation that must be cleared up right away," replied Andrew.

"The Boss!" exclaimed Jimmy, "who's your Boss?"

"Why, who do you think Jimmy," replied Andrew, "it's HIM."

"Him," asked Jimmy, "do you mean – HIM himself?"

"That's right, Him, Gabriel!" replied Andrew. "You'd better get straight on to this one, because somewhere on earth, someone has just prayed and said 'In the name of God' so it's more than urgent, it's immediate. HE is on a promise of His Word."

"What's all this then, is it something I should have learned in church?" asked Jimmy.

"Yes," replied Andrew, "but don't worry, not many churches down there teach the right things about HIM or what he stands for. Otherwise, we wouldn't have half the problems that we have now, people not knowing where to go or what to do when their time comes to cross over."

Andrew sounded quite disgusted at the lack of basic teaching in the earthly church. Jimmy was taken by surprise, as he always thought that going to church was just something you did to be seen doing, to make you look like you were a better person.

"Why doesn't someone tell the people what they should know, then," asked Jimmy, "'cause they don't all read the Bible, do they?"

"The trouble was, that as man developed the gospel to match in with what they wanted the people to know, a lot of the important stuff was left out. The original Gospels and writings are still hidden away from sight, gathering dust in church vaults like the Vatican, and Westminster Abbey, because they would change the whole concept of Christianity, as they know it. People would live together in love and peace, and would have special powers to do miracles and healings. But look what they have; they go to a building on a Sunday and park their big precious cars outside, and just to be seen going to church like a real goodie, goodie person. And are they any better off for being there? No!"

"What do you want me to do then, Andrew?" asked Jimmy, cautiously, as he could see that anger was rising in his face.

"There is a ghost on earth, he's been haunting this house for some twenty or so years and is becoming a right pain for the inhabitants," replied Andrew, "go down there and get him brought over, because he's started throwing things about now and someone might get killed accidentally."

"Why would that matter, accidentally?" asked Jimmy.

"Because it causes problems up here," said Andrew, "we would have to re-schedule the life again to make up the difference. Anyway, that's something that doesn't concern you at this stage, just get down there and bring him up to me."

"Anything you say, boss," said Jimmy and looked at the details for the house. He was there in the blinking of an eye, standing outside a beautiful Georgian manner house at the end of a little village in Surrey. Everything looked perfect from the outside, nice long driveway, two garages, superb lawns and gardens. "If this is the house of a Christian family, where did I go wrong?" said Jimmy to himself.

"They are Christians," said the voice of Andrew, "and they have done a lot of good work with the under-privileged. Some Christians actually do the work that they are supposed to do."

"Fine by me," said Jimmy, "I will do my utmost to solve this problem for you."

Jimmy went to the front door and knocked, standing there in his black suit, white shirt and black tie. The door opened slowly, by a young woman. She looked to be about twenty-five years old, slim, short blonde hair and nice figure. She was hardly the type of person that Jimmy was expecting to see.

"Can I help you?" she said.

"Well, it's more a question of, can I help you," replied Jimmy, "you see, I've heard that you're having trouble with a ghost."

The young woman was quite surprised at the words, and shouted for her husband to come quickly.

"What's wrong darling?" said her husband, a young, handsome man in his late twenties, and by all accounts, very prosperous in whatever it was that he did for a living.

"This man says he knows that we have a ghost," she replied.

"Who are you?" asked her husband, "and who told you these stories?"

"I've been sent in answer to the prayer of someone that has been in touch with you," replied Jimmy, "and I've come to relieve you of an unwanted spirit."

The man and woman looked at each other, then he said cautiously, "You'd better come in."

They led Jimmy into the most amazing house that he had ever seen, nothing was out of place, and what was in its place, was absolutely unbelievable! It was like a museum full of fine arts and treasures.

"This is very nice," remarked Jimmy as he looked all around the walls and ceilings.

"We've both worked very hard to get it how we wanted it," replied the man, "but most of it was left to me by my father when he died."

"Crossed over to the other side," corrected Jimmy.

"What?" asked the young man.

"The proper phrasing is 'crossed over' to the other side," answered Jimmy without thinking.

"Are you some sort of medium?" asked the young woman, "because we don't believe in all that mumbo-jumbo stuff, we're actually Christians."

"No way, I'm not a medium, I'm ..." Jimmy stopped short to think about his answer, what should he tell them?

"Tell them the truth, Jimmy, and they'll believe you," said Andrew's voice, "but get on with it."

"No, I'm not a medium, young lady, I'm actually the angel that comes to collect people and take them across to the other side," replied Jimmy.

They both stopped dead in their tracks, looked at each other with a very concerned look, and then turned to Jimmy.

"Is this some kind of sick joke you've been put up to?" asked the man, with a great deal of annoyance in his voice, "because we've had people playing pranks on us before. Just who are you and what do you want?" he snapped.

"Well," began Jimmy, "if it's proof you want I suppose I'd better give it to you before you call the police or something. I don't need to ask your names, they're Derek and Janice McNiece. Yes, you are Christians, and yes I am here to answer the prayer that your friend Ian Brown prayed with you in this very room. It was 11.00 p.m. last night, and you Janice, were wearing the same clothes that you have on tonight except for the underwear of course, and you Derek, smoked a nice cigar before retiring to bed. Do you require any further proof?"

They looked at each other then Derek spoke up.

"You could have been told all that by somebody except that nobody knows that I like a cigar now and then, even though I'm a Christian!"

"Not to worry," said Jimmy with a voice of authority, "you won't go to hell just because you smoke, but you might smell like you've been there."

That made both of them smile, but they were very uneasy at entertaining this strange man in their home. After all, he could just be a clever criminal who was casing the place, and would come back later with his gang.

"I'm still not convinced that you're who you say you are," said Janice, "after all, I've never seen an angel, so I don't know what one looks like anyway."

"Trust me," replied Jimmy, "I am here to help, but if it's silly proof you want and not belief in my word, then I am to reveal things to you that will convince and clear the situation. You have been trying for a baby for three years now, and you have had one miscarriage. The next time you and Derek go together you will conceive and have a boy child."

Janice looked astonished at Jimmy, then at Derek.

"Is this some cruel joke?" retorted Derek, "you're upsetting my wife with all this claptrap and nonsense."

"You Christians take some convincing!" said Jimmy, "but here goes!"

Jimmy looked them in the face, turned, and walked through the wall into the next room. He came back through the wall carrying a small cigar box from off the table.

As Derek and Janice stood there with mouths wide open, Jimmy offered Derek a cigar. It was obviously too big to have been in the box, and it lit itself as Jimmy put it in Derek's mouth and pushed his jaw back up.

Janice collapsed on the floor; Derek blew out a big cloud of smoke.

"Wow," said Derek, "that's got to be the best cigar I've ever tasted!"

Jimmy nodded and turned Derek's attention to Janice, who was just coming round from her faint.

She looked up and saw Derek with this large cigar poking out of his mouth.

They both agreed that Jimmy could help, and apologised for their mistrust.

"Don't worry," said Jimmy, "that is, until you see me coming to take you across."

This was seen as a joke and a bit of light-hearted fun, which joined the three of them in a weird kind of friendship.

They told him that the ghost appeared, usually, around 12.15 a.m. At first it was just 'feelings' and noises, but now it had got to the stage where objects and furniture were starting to be moved about the rooms.

"Well if you don't mind, I'll just sit here and wait till he appears, and you can get on with whatever you are doing," said Jimmy. "Do you actually know who this ghost used to be?"

Janice replied, as Derek was still enjoying the big cigar.

"We are led to believe that he used to live here before we moved in, about ten years ago. Apparently, he is supposed to have murdered his wife and buried her in the garden somewhere, but the police dug it all up and found nothing. They never found his wife either. That's why we think he's never moved on, because of what will be waiting for him. Or as some people think, he wants to find his wife first before he can leave."

"Well he's leaving tonight, with or without her," said Jimmy.

"You know when you said about the prayer, and praying in God's Name made it priority?" asked Derek. "Well, does that go for everything that you say like that?"

"Yes, within reason," answered Jimmy the great authority on scripture, who only went to church because he was sent by his father, "so long as you're praying in the will of God and not for something out of context, or something that will be wrong for you."

They both looked amazed at his frank answer, as if to put that in their memory for next time they wanted something.

"Oh no!" said Janice, "we've got guests coming for dinner tonight, they'll see you too, won't they?"

"Of course they will, Janice," replied Jimmy, "but you will pass me off as your caterer, and I will cook your dinner for you, tonight."

"Can you do that?" asked Derek, "can angels cook and do?"

"I am at liberty to use whatever powers I have to use to get my job done," said Jimmy, "and tonight will be a night to remember!"

The couple went upstairs and dressed to receive their guests, who arrived in two cars at 7.00 p.m. Janice welcomed them and sat them down with a glass of wine and continued the conversation while Derek checked on the caterer in the kitchen. Jimmy was nowhere to be seen, and then he re-appeared in front of Derek.

"Wow, that made me jump, err ... I don't even know your name, what do I call you?"

"My name is James De'Ath, Derek, pleased to be of service to you," replied Jimmy with a smile. "Drink? Cigar? What can I get you while we're waiting?"

Derek looked around the kitchen, it was spotlessly clean, but that's how Janice kept it, clean! There was no sign of any cooking, no smell, no smoke, nothing!

"You said that you would prepare our dinner tonight, James, and you've done nothing," said Derek, "and our guests are already here! What are we going to do? It will take hours to prepare a meal at this time! They are really important friends of ours, too!"

"You only have to ring for the butler and your meal will be served, my dear friend, Derek," replied Jimmy

"But there's nothing ready, can't you understand what I am saying?" said Derek in a little above normal volume.

Just then the kitchen door opened and Janice came in to see what was happening. She immediately sensed what was wrong, as she couldn't smell anything cooking either!

"Oh no," she said, "tell me this is all a dream!"

"Janice," said Jimmy, "where is your faith now? Do you remember the loaves and fishes?"

"Yes I remember loaves and I remember fishes, but that was in those times and it was Jesus Christ who was at the helm in the storm and the billows …" Then she fainted onto the floor.

"Oh my God!" shouted Derek, "look what you've done now!"

"Yes it is your God, Derek," said Jimmy, "but where is your trust and your faith in Him?"

Derek looked up from the floor as he picked up Janice on her recovery, a little bit startled but still worried.

"I don't know what you mean, Mr James whoever you are," said Derek, "what am I supposed to think or do, I just don't know!"

Janice looked at them both. "If you say that this will be all right, then I will trust you as an angel of God."

Derek looked at her in amazement. "What!" he shouted, "you're ready to trust this person or 'angel' whom we have never clapped eyes on before, with guests in our house too!"

Janice looked at Jimmy, who shrugged his shoulders, and then she looked at Derek.

"We are supposed to be Christians, Derek, and look at us! You were highly convinced when he gave you a cigar, weren't you?"

They thought for a moment, then realised! "The guests! We've left them on their own for nearly fifteen minutes! What will they think of us?"

Jimmy smiled, "Don't worry, they won't even realise you've been away from them. Just go back in and start the conversation where you left off, and leave the rest to me. Now both of you, have faith, and GO!"

They left the kitchen and went back into the lounge, where nobody seemed to moving or talking, they were sat there like dummies in a clothes shop. When Janice and Derek sat down, they all came back to normal and talked on as though nothing had happened. The couple looked at each other and agreed to trust Jimmy.

Before Derek could offer anyone another glass of wine, Jimmy appeared in the doorway, dressed like a butler, and announced that dinner was served in the dining room. Everyone stood up and headed towards the door where Jimmy the butler ushered them into the dining room. It had an enormous table with ten chairs around it, all in a beautiful dark walnut finish.

The chairs were obviously Chippendale, and the magnificent table was inlaid with various colours of wood and gold. Above it, hung a crystal chandelier of about six feet in diameter, glittering with light and sparkling with jewels. Around the walls were several old masters that were clearly identifiable to anyone. The table was laid with silver dishes and plates containing the most delicious looking food imaginable, freshly cooked and steaming hot. At one end was a serving table, with two large roasts awaiting carving!

Derek was speechless, but had to grab hold of Janice before she fainted again. Pleased? Oh yes they were pleased, it was just that they didn't have a dining room just here in their house and they don't own such a table and all the decorations!

Jimmy nodded to Derek and winked at Janice. "This way sir, madam, you are sitting here," said Jimmy, as he pulled a chair out for Janice and made one come out on its own for Derek. They were seated at the head of the table of course.

Janice noticed that all the guests were seated in exactly the right places, but then, they all had place names written in gold on their napkins!

Jimmy served the wine, the delicacies, the starters and all with such a convincing manner, that nobody suspected anything. He nearly slipped up when he was serving the wine though, as he filled everyone's glass from the one, single bottle. There were eight guests and some had white wine and some had red!

Jimmy clicked his fingers and a second waiter appeared from a doorway at the end of the room. He began to assist with serving up the main course, and took orders and instructions from Jimmy at a beckoning or a gesture with his hand. Derek and Janice were feeling a bit calmer by now, and the wine had started working too! Jimmy came around to Janice with the wine, and said, "Getting into the spirit of things now, madam, pardon the pun?"

"Yes, James," she whispered, "but where did all this come from, and whose is it?"

"It's only on loan from a stately home in Derbyshire, they won't miss it for one night," replied Jimmy.

She smiled back, but didn't know whether he was joking or not.

"James," whispered Derek, "who's the additional waiting staff, is he from an agency?"

"No," replied Jimmy quietly, "he's a spirit that's passing over, and I've got him to help me out for a while till we're done here. He was a waiter at a stately home, you know!"

Derek swallowed and carried on with a conversation with a guest at the side of him.

The evening went so well, that no one realised how late it was, except Jimmy. The clock had already struck midnight and nobody seemed to have any inclination to be moving off home. Jimmy told Janice and Derek that he would have to leave them in the capable hands of his waiter friend, while he went to hunt a ghost. They pretended not to be bothered about what he had said to them, as one of the guests might overhear him say it.

"Hunting for a ghost, Derek?" said the man. "What's this then?"

"We are having a little bother from a past resident of our house, in that he keeps coming back!" owned up Derek.

"Wow," he replied, "and this butler of yours, by the way, I must borrow him and his mate there, the next time we have a bash at our house, he's gone off to find your ghost?"

"Yes," said Derek, not too loud so that the rest of the guests would hear him, "he's a 'ghost hunter' when he's not a butler, or should I say, well, he's got a job on the side."

Derek realised that he'd made the situation worse by not knowing what to say, and saying anything was worse than saying nothing.

Then the man who he'd been talking to stood and announced to the other guests, "I say everyone, Derek and Janice have got a ghost in their lovely house, and their butler has gone to hunt it down! What say we all tag along and see what happens, what?"

Derek stood to his feet quickly, "No, no, it's all right, James the butler will sort it out, and he might like it better if we stayed out of his way."

It was too late for Derek, the guests had agreed that this was the ultimate climax to the best dinner party they had ever been to in their lives, and they weren't going to miss this!

They all stood up and left the table, rushing into the lounge to find the butler. Jimmy had been concentrating on his approaching ghost and didn't notice that the guests were arriving behind him until they were all present. What should he do now? Leave it and come back again, or carry on?

Andrew gave him the answer in a split second and Jimmy turned around to his audience.

"In a few moments ladies and gentlemen, there will be an apparition in that doorway. Please, all of you stay calm, it won't hurt you in any way," announced Jimmy.

Although excited, they were all very scared, and hairs even stood up on top of the bald heads of two of the men!

They watched as a shape appeared in the doorway. It was a man who looked to be in his fifties, clean-shaven and dressed in a black suit. Jimmy recognised the trappings of a funeral suit, always the black one!

The guests took a step back, leaving Jimmy way out in front of them. As the man approached, he saw Jimmy and recognised him for who he was. "Why are you here, Death?" he asked.

"For you my friend, to take you back with me," replied Jimmy.

"I'm not ready to go with you, I've got to find my wife, she's left me here," moaned the man.

"You have no choice," said Jimmy, "you're going across right now, wife or no wife. Anyway, you know where your wife is, you killed her fifty years ago and put her body in the old chimney behind this beautiful oak wall panelling, remember? Remember how drunk you used to get and start hitting her about? That's when you had the police digging up all the gardens. You knew where she was all the time, and you just sat here scared stiff until you died of malnutrition and hypothermia. So don't give us all that wailing about how dear she was to you, she's alive on the other side and you're dead here!"

Jimmy and the spirit disappeared to the rapturous applause of the guests, apart from two women who had fainted.

Derek and Janice just stood there and looked on, unbelievable happenings, right in their front room. The guests decided that they had definitely just attended the very best dinner party of their lives, and after making generous donations to the charity that Derek and Janice were supporting, they all got into their large cars and left.

One of the women came back after five minutes, as she had left her clutch bag at the table. Janice told her that she would go and get it for her. She opened the double doors to what was the magnificent dining hall, only to find that it was now their cosy little study again. Everything was gone! The table, the chairs, the paintings, everything was gone and the room was just like it had been when Jimmy first arrived.

On the armchair in the corner was the woman's bag, so Janice grabbed it and rushed back into the lounge to give it to her.

When everything was quiet again, Janice took Derek by the hand and led him into the study, which was still their little study. He looked as if he had just woken up from a dream, and everything was back to normal.

They asked themselves, did we really have a magnificent dinner, and all that posh furniture, or did we imagine it?

"I'm full and couldn't eat another crumb," said Derek, "so we must have eaten!"

"That's what James said, isn't it? Remember? He said remember the loaves and fishes," said Janice.

"Yes, when everyone had eaten they were so full, that they collected up all the crumbs, no one could eat even another crumb!" agreed Derek.

They looked at each other and then prayed and thanked God for a miracle. That had really strengthened their faith, and when Derek looked at the cheques from his guests, his faith was even stronger!

The next day, when Derek went to the bank where he was the manager, he deposited the cheques into the account for the charity that helped children in need. He also contacted the police and a builder to examine the old chimney, where they found the body of a woman.

Later that week, he was at a district meeting of bank managers, just near Birmingham, and met a colleague named Martin Coney. Over lunch, they talked about their mundane lives at the banks, and Derek told him about the strange happenings at his home, to rid them of a ghost. Martin listened with great interest, as he had heard the stories of breezes in the cemetery and candles being blown out at his mother's house. Martin offered to pay for the pub lunch that they had just enjoyed, and as he pulled out his wallet a couple of cards and photographs fell onto the floor. Derek picked them up for him and noticed the photographs.

"Oh that's my mother with my wife and kids, and this one is my father," said Martin.

"Why did I think that I could tell you about the dinner party, it must have been fate, Martin!" said Derek, bewildered.

"Why, what's up old chap," said Martin, "you look like you've seen a ghost!"

CHAPTER NINE

Children Too? No Andrew, Please

Jimmy went to see Andrew and received quite a commendation for the handling of the haunted house, apart from the fact that he had an uninvited audience. But Jimmy got the job done anyway.

"Will HE know that we've done the job, then, Andrew?" asked Jimmy.

"Of course," replied Andrew, "he was probably there with you for some of the time."

Jimmy thought for a moment.

"*Would* he have been, do you think, even while I was doing all that stage management of the dinner and suchlike?" said Jimmy.

"Oh yes, he likes anything amusing like that, you know. He's not stiff and starchy like the vicar of an old cathedral," replied Andrew.

Jimmy looked amazed and then said, "Gabriel has a sense of humour?"

"Of course," replied Andrew, "where did you think that sense of humour came from, something man thought up for his own entertainment? It all gets sent from here down to there, and that did too! Mind you, he doesn't care much for Jewish jokes so watch your thoughts."

"I can't get my head round this, Andrew," said Jimmy, "I've always been led to believe that God and Gabriel are like, you know, right up there and we are totally different right down to earth. Yet you are saying that my God and the Angel Gabriel have a sense of humour!"

"It's true, Jimmy, and I know it must be hard to believe after all the things you've heard as a boy in Sunday school," said Andrew. "You should have been taught that God is Love, and He loves His people to be happy with all the things that He has given them.

"I went to the earth plane on a Sunday once, on some urgent business, and I passed by a church that had just started to empty out after the service. If you had seen the miserable faces on those people, you wouldn't have wanted to become a Christian! In fact, it's those kind of people that turn many others away! Undeterred, I went to one of those Methodist type chapels to see if it was any better, and it wasn't! Gabriel wanted to have a laugh with me, saying that all were welcome in a church, so he asked me to go dressed as a tramp!"

"Dressed as tramp!" wailed Jimmy, "I bet you were very popular, weren't you?"

"They actually gave me a small amount of coins and told me to leave!" replied Andrew, "and Gabriel was quite upset with them for that."

"What did he do?" asked Jimmy.

"Well," replied Andrew, "their precious church burnt down a few weeks later."

"Did HE do that!" asked Jimmy, all excited at the sound of revenge.

"I'm not sure," replied Andrew, attempting to put a damper on Jimmy's enthusiasm, "apparently the central heating boiler went wrong. That's all he said."

"I bet that taught them a lesson though, didn't it?" said Jimmy.

"Not really, they just held fairs and sales to raise enough money to build another church," said Andrew, "and it's just as it used to be again."

"Well," said Jimmy, "can't he ..."

"Enough of this, you have work to do for me," said Andrew, changing the subject quickly, "and this is your next assignment."

Jimmy looked at the address and the name, but looked back at Andrew with an ashen face.

"You can't be serious, Andrew" he said, "This is a three year old child!"

"So," replied Andrew, "how do think a three year old child will find his way to me if you don't go and show him? He would end up running all over the place and becoming another haunting spirit."

"I can't do this one, mate," said Jimmy, "I had children of my own on earth!"

"Jimmy, you are the perfect person for the job then, you will understand the mind of a child better, won't you?" replied Andrew.

"I see what you mean," said Jimmy, "I'm straight on it." Jimmy was back on earth in the twinkling of an eye, standing just outside a large house near the coast. It was one of those strangely designed houses, with the bedrooms on the ground floor and a lounge upstairs. "Odd," thought Jimmy, as he peered through the keyhole, "I wonder, who would live in a house like this, it's over to you, Jimmy."

There was a party going on, just a few friends and relatives getting together for a birthday bash. Jimmy changed into light blue slacks and a polo neck shirt, very casual, just like all the other guests.

He walked in through the wall near to the table where the drinks were, and helped himself to a small glass of wine. Looking around the room, he quickly noticed the birthday cards on the mantlepiece, which were for the man of the house.

"Oh, at least it's not the little fellow's birthday," thought Jimmy, "but this will be a birthday to remember for this couple!"

Some of the other guests came in to get a drink, and chatted to Jimmy as though he were some friend or relative. Then the birthday boy himself came in, and Jimmy smiled and wished him "many happy returns", and then realised just what he had said. But what else do you say to someone on his or her birthday, even if you know that it will bring back all the bad memories of a disaster each year. Worse than that, though, as Jimmy looked at the young man he thought he recognised who he was, and in fact he did know him. It was Peter, Gerry's friend from the war zone filming!

"What am I going to do now?" thought Jimmy.

"Do the best you can for him of course," replied Andrew's voice.

Jimmy wandered outside to the enormous swimming pool in the garden, it was just like the one he remembered back in his old town, but that was a Leisure Centre! There were people everywhere, sitting, swimming, drinking and eating.

There was also a large number of children running around and jumping into the pool, screaming and yelling with the fun of it all. Jimmy's smile turned to a face of anguish when he realised that the boy that he had been sent to take was there, and he looked just like Martin when he was three years old, it was Peter's son. Jimmy sat down in a chair at the poolside to watch the scene for a while, gathering his thoughts of bygone days and happy moments.

"Jimmy," said Andrew, "I know this is difficult but it is the time. It's no good putting it out of your mind either. The man, Peter, will be at the pool in a moment and you must make sure that he sees the little one in the shallow end. He won't be able to do anything because it's already too late, then take the child by the hand."

"O.K. Andrew," said Jimmy, "but this is really cutting me up inside, and yet I'm a spirit! How can that be? I thought that we had no senses after we had died?"

"Spirits still care and feel for people," said Andrew, "that's why some of them want to attend those séances to get a message of comfort through to their relatives."

"Yes, I see what you mean," said Jimmy sipping his wine in the sunshine, "I've been to one of them, haven't I?"

"Oh yes," said Andrew, "and what a disaster you made of it too! Anyway, how's the wine?"

Jimmy smiled, as he knew that Andrew would love a glass of this!

Peter came out to the poolside with a glass of wine in his hand, and put it on the table by the side of Jimmy. He didn't recognise Jimmy because he had only seen him for a very short while some years ago in Afghanistan, and with all the action at the time, and all the action now, he never made the connection.

"Don't let any of the kids get their hands on this," he said to Jimmy as he prepared to dive into the pool.

"Hey Peter!" called Jimmy, "what's up with Mikey in the shallow end, does he like swimming under water?"

Peter looked across, "My God! Mikey!" he shouted, and ran down the side of the pool. He jumped in and picked up his little son out of the water, placing him carefully on the poolside. Two other people assisted with mouth-to-mouth and heart massage, while they waited for the ambulance to arrive. Ten minutes later, while the paramedics were assessing the little boy's state, Jimmy held out his hand and took hold of Mikey's hand, and his spirit sat with Jimmy as they watched for a moment.

"Hi Mikey," said Jimmy, "I'm Jimmy, and I've been sent to take you to a nice place, where you can have a lot of fun."

"You look like my Uncle Jimmy," said Mikey, a bright, blonde-haired and blue-eyed little boy, smiling into Jimmy's face, and showing no fear at all, like children do.

"You have an Uncle Jimmy?" asked Jimmy.

"Well, he's not really my uncle, but he knows my dad from before I was born, along with Uncle Gerry."

Jimmy's face turned grey as he looked at the father, crying over his dead son's body by the pool.

"Peter," he thought, "Peter, Gerry's friend."

He hadn't seen Peter since Afghanistan, and here he was, living in this beautiful house near the sea. Gerry had certainly looked after his war correspondents and paid them what they were due to. One of the men who had tried to help little Mikey stood up and tried to comfort Peter. It was Gerry. Alongside him was Marie.

"I'm sorry, Jimmy," said Andrew, who was now standing beside Jimmy and Mikey, "this must be difficult I know, but I didn't want you to come back to me and find out that this had happened without you knowing. Believe me, it's not good when a child is involved, but this will make you stronger for the future."

"But why?" murmured Jimmy to Andrew, in a bewildered voice, "why Peter's little boy?"

"Jimmy, he has never been a well child, he has a chronic heart disease caused by his mother's addiction to drugs in her earlier years, and he would have died long before he was an adult. Peter knew about his wife's condition before they married, in fact, it was Peter who got her off the drugs, with some help from Gerry. They always knew that he was not a fit child, but they didn't expect to lose him to an accident in their swimming pool. Don't worry too much, they will try for another baby in a year's time and it will be a perfect little boy."

"There's my son and his wife, can I talk to them?" asked Jimmy.

"Not really a good idea at this moment, Jimmy," replied Andrew, "let them get *this* upset out of their minds, as I am sure that they wouldn't appreciate seeing your ghost at the same time, would they?"

Jimmy looked for a moment, and watched as Gerry and Marie hugged the two parents, tears rolling down everyone's faces. The party was over, but it would never be forgotten.

Gerry, as usual, had fixed up two small cameras around the pool to film the whole of the party, which would be edited later and the best parts kept as a record.

"Come on Uncle Jimmy," piped up little Mikey, "you said we were going to go somewhere and have some fun, and I feel really well now that my pains have gone!"

Andrew looked at Jimmy, "See what I mean mate?"

"Come on then big boy," said Jimmy, taking the little fellow by the hand, "wave goodbye to your mum and dad, and let's go to see Uncle Andrew's place, right up there beyond that blue sky."

"Goodbye mummy, goodbye daddy," shouted little Mikey, "see you soon!"

Jimmy had never seen Mikey, Peter's son before he died, but it was obvious that Peter had told him the tale of the rescue from the terrorists. He must have shown him some photographs, too.

Jimmy, Andrew and little Mikey walked through the patio doors and vanished from the scene, and once processed, Jimmy took the little lad for a wander around the beautiful places on the next level after the earth plane as Andrew called it.

"There are plenty of other little children here for you to play with," said Jimmy, "and lots of nice things to do and see."

"When will mummy and daddy be able to come here, Uncle Jimmy?" asked little Mikey.

"When it's their time," replied Jimmy, "when it's their time."

After the funeral service for little Mikey a week later, Marie remembered about the two cameras that had filmed the party, and asked Gerry if he had edited the film yet. The pair of them sat down in front of their television and watched the escapades of the guests at Peter's party. It made them laugh to see and remember the antics of some of the people there, who did not know about the cameras. Then, in one shot from the camera facing the patio doors, they saw a greyed image of what looked like a guest coming out to the pool, carrying a drink.

Gerry replayed it several times, and couldn't understand what had happened to the colour. Then he suggested to Marie that he would take it to the television studios where he worked, and let their engineers take a look.

The rest of the film was not too amusing, as it showed Peter trying to revive his little son.

About a week later, Gerry came home from work at the television centre and had the tape of the party in his hand. He found Marie and told her to come and look what the engineers had done to the film.

"Oh, was there a problem with the actual film or camera, then?" asked Marie.

"No," replied Gerry, sounding somewhat exciting and annoyed, "just take a look at it now that they have done their little bits to it, and spruced up the colour element in it. They've done some reduction in the gamma and up lit the back colour, and all sorts of things, but you will not believe what I have just seen!"

"Oh, what?" asked Marie.

"My father!" retorted Gerry. "It definitely looks like him in the shot, and there's more."

"Don't be daft, Gerry, your father died a few years ago, how can he be at Peter's party?" asked Marie.

"Just watch this!" said Gerry, and the two of them stared in disbelief as the film showed Jimmy walking out of the patio doors with a glass of wine. The glass of wine was, of course, prominent in the uncut film, but you couldn't see who was carrying it. Gerry thought at first that it was something to do with the sun, shining onto the doors, but now he knew different.

They saw Jimmy sitting beside the pool, smiling and sipping his wine, talking with Peter as well! And they saw him vanish with Mikey and another person. Marie and Gerry couldn't believe it, but after a few re-runs of the tape, they saw the whole thing for what it was. Gerry's father had come for Mikey! This helped to make them feel better, in a way, and more able to deal with the accident of Mikey's death. A family get together was arranged, including Peter and his wife, and the tape was played to them all. Hazel cried tears of sorrow and joy, as she had already had her own meeting with Jimmy, at the séance. Martin related the story about his colleague and the mysterious butler, which all seemed to fit together now, and more clearly.

"It appears," announced Martin, "that our father has a new job in his after-life, that of guiding people to the other side. It must be quite a change from laying gas pipes."

Hazel told them about the séance and that she had spoken with Jimmy, and now they had no reason to disbelieve her. Marie said that she had believed Hazel's account about the cemetery and the séance, but this was something else!

"But what does all this mean," asked Marie, "why are we seeing these things and knowing all this stuff about spirits and ghostly goings on?"

"Jimmy is telling us that he is all right," said Hazel, "and now I am not afraid to cross over to the other side, because I know he's there and waiting for me, for us, and it's beautiful, don't you think?"

The family were quite taken up with all this, and it did seem as if Jimmy had given them some kind of hope, whilst giving them a good reason to bond together as a family. He had always stood firm on family values and morals. Nothing ever came before any member of the family in his eyes, and no problem was too big to be dealt with by the family. His usual motto was 'United we stand' as a family!

Peter and his wife felt like part of the Coney household too, and as Andrew had predicted, one year later they would be expecting a new arrival.

CHAPTER TEN

Commuter Rail Crash

"Jimmy," said Andrew, "you have got another commendation for your work, for dealing with people you know and children. As you have found, these are two very difficult areas, and you have done it."

"Well, it wasn't easy in the least," replied Jimmy, "but I know about the end product of the accident with little Mikey, and I understand that all things do work out for the good of people in the end."

"Of course," agreed Andrew, "but it doesn't seem like that to the people on the earth plane for a lot of the time, does it? They cause bad things to happen in their lives, and then they want someone to blame for it!"

"I know," agreed Jimmy, "done a bit of that myself over the years."

"What are you like on trains?" asked Andrew.

"How do you mean, diesel or steam?" said Jimmy. "I've never been a train spotter, and I've always had a van or a car."

"No, no," replied Andrew, "can you travel on a train?"

"Yes of course, I can travel on anything, in anything, and drive just about anything from a moped to a cruiser," said Jimmy.

"Good," said Andrew, "then you won't mind doing me a 'multiple' for the next assignment, will you?"

"Multiple?" quizzed Jimmy, "that sounds like another one of your training exercises, Andrew, pardon the pun! What's it all about then, and has someone done one of these before?"

"Oh yes," replied Andrew, "many times in the past. Why, only last year we had several really bad train crashes, and hundreds of people crossed over from them, sometimes more than one hundred at a time!"

"Where's the one that you want me to do then, and when?" asked Jimmy.

"Just south of London, a commuter train full of people going to work in the city," said Andrew.

"Why?" asked Jimmy, "why kill all those innocent people on their way to earn a living to keep their families?"

"Man has been given the right of personal choice," said Andrew, "he can make any invention do what he wants it to do, be it for his good or his destruction. Sometimes, the things that are made for the good of the world are not driven properly and lead to accidents."

"I see your point," agreed Jimmy, " when and where?"

"You'd better get straight down to the station, Jimmy, it's already leaving and it's only ten minutes late today," said Andrew. "That's a first for this train. Watch out for the next station and then the red signal light. The driver will go straight through, and after two earth time minutes he will hit the express train coming down the same line, head on!"

"Why?" asked Jimmy. "Why doesn't the driver stop at the red light, like I had to do when I was driving my car?"

"They have invented all sorts of reasons on the earth plane for that, but it's all down to bad driving in my book," replied Andrew with shoulders shrugged in disgust.

Jimmy "beamed" himself down, as he had come to call this new method of getting to places, and was standing at the end of a carriage holding onto a grab rail. It was full of people who were on their way to work in the city of London, most of them reading newspapers or chatting with their fellow passengers.

"It all seems so pointless doesn't it?" thought Jimmy, "all these people rushing to jobs in the city and one man is allowed to take it all from them. Why can't I do something about it other than just wait for the smash?"

"There is nothing you can do in this case, Jimmy, it's all on the cards for happening like I said," came Andrew's voice. "Still, if you want to try something, go ahead and have a go, I'm sure I can give you the green light on this, pardon the pun."

"It's you with that phrase!" said Jimmy, "you've got me at it as well now. I'm going to have a try at stopping the train, Andrew, I feel it must be worth one chance to save lives."

Jimmy 'beamed' himself up the track to where the red light was shining brightly in the grey light of the early morning, and thought for a moment.

"What if I make this light into two red lights," he thought, "then the driver will definitely see it, won't he?"

Jimmy concentrated on the light and it appeared as two glowing in the morning mist. Just then, he saw the train coming down the tracks towards him, and the lights. The driver took no notice and went straight through onto the next track. Jimmy was astonished and beamed himself back into the train. He had only just got there when there was one almighty big bang and the carriages turned upside down. He was still standing, of course, but everyone else was thrown about everywhere in the train. Jimmy looked in amazement and horror. A few minutes ago this was a train full of people going to work, and now it was a disaster!

Then some of them started to come out, grey spirits standing beside their crumpled bodies, wondering what had happened.

One man looked at Jimmy in bewilderment and said, "Why are you standing there, unhurt, and what happened to the train?"

Jimmy tried to explain quickly: "There's been a very bad crash, and you are now crossing over to the other side. You're actually dead."

The man looked around as all the people in the carriage stood up, grey spirits amidst the rubble and twisted wreckage. They were all asking the same question, so this prompted Jimmy to make a special announcement over the trains public address system. The system didn't really work, Jimmy made that happen, but it was what the people were waiting for, directions and advice.

"Will you please come to this end of the carriage and through this door on my right. There has been a very bad accident and the train has crashed, and you are all going to be safe when you have crossed over with me," said Jimmy.

The passengers had many questions to ask, like, Can I call my wife; can I see if my colleague is all right; I need my laptop; can I use my mobile phone!

Jimmy guided them through the door to where Andrew was waiting, and then did the same thing in each carriage that was damaged, on both trains!

Hundreds of souls crossed over in one go, and Jimmy found himself becoming quite busy with the directing of such a large operation. Andrew always coped with any number of new arrivals; after all, he had been doing this for many years, nearly six hundred by all account.

As Jimmy passed through one wrecked carriage, he heard the murmur of someone who must have been trapped. He stopped and looked around, to find the body of a young woman entangled in the remains of her seat. Jimmy made himself body and appeared as one of the paramedics, complete with green helmet and jump suit.

"Are you all right?" he said to her "What's your name?"

"Help me," she groaned, "I'm Claire, and I think I've broken my arm and a leg, but I can't get out, I'm stuck!"

"We'll have you out of there in a minute," said Jimmy, "just stay calm and I'll fetch help."

"No! Don't leave me!" she cried, "I don't want to be left in here on my own with all these dead bodies, and I'm frightened."

Jimmy had two choices: Go and fetch some help or do something with his limited powers, but which one would be best. Just then, he heard what sounded like a hissing noise from under the train. This was the buffet car, and that was the gas cylinder rupturing! "No time to waste" thought Jimmy, "this calls for a 'Coney' special!"

He put his hands on the metal that was trapping the young woman and began to pull it away, but it wouldn't bend into a position where he could free her, safely. His helmet fell off and clattered around the wreckage, and it made the young woman feel distressed, as she thought that the train was moving. She was right! The train was beginning to slide down the twenty-foot embankment, onto another main line!

"Andrew!" shouted Jimmy, "I need some help down here, and quick!"

Without a word, standing by Jimmy's side was a huge man who looked like a Roman Gladiator.

"Who the bloody hell are you?" snapped Jimmy. "Not one of Andrew's jokes, are you?"

"Stand back, Mr James," said the big man, and he lifted the chair and table up and off the woman, as though it was made of paper!

"My name is Samson," he replied, "but my friends call me, Samson."

Jimmy was somewhat stunned as the big man grinned, and then disappeared.

"What was Andrew playing at now?" he thought, "but it worked!"

Then the train began to slide a bit more, and the young woman got halfway to her feet and clung onto Jimmy's suit.

"Get me out of here, please, Mr James," she said, as she had heard the other man call him that, "I think my waters have just broken too!"

Jimmy was speechless! What should he do now! He helped her to her feet and then carried her out of the carriage. Placing her firmly on the ground he found some seat cushions and towels and made her as comfortable as he could.

The rest of the paramedics, police and fire crews were further down the tracks, as this carriage had become disconnected and looked safe. They also thought that there was no one in it, as most people would have moved back to their seats when the train had left the last station. This pregnant young woman was travelling in the buffet car to be out of the crush of the rest of the people on the train.

Jimmy shouted down the tracks for help, but no one heard him above all the noise.

"Mr James, I think my baby is coming!" screamed Claire.

"Don't panic, this is an everyday thing, you will be all right, Claire, trust me," said Jimmy.

Then he pulled her skirt up over her waist and removed her panties. There was the baby's head already coming out of its mother with great impatience!

Jimmy told her to push, and pant, and push, and pant, and push and pant until eventually a healthy little baby was wriggling in his hands. He reached into his suit and made a pair of scissors and two clamps appear, along with a wrap for the baby and bandages from his first aid bag. After cutting the cord and placing the placenta in a plastic bag, he propped her up and gently handed her the baby. He told her that he had to get an ambulance for her, and wouldn't be long before he came back. She smiled and nodded, and carried on nursing her new child.

Jimmy beamed down to where an ambulance was parked and looked around for the paramedics. They were just returning with a stretcher from one of the other carriages, and Jimmy told them to come straight away, telling them where his patient was lying. They said that they would come straight down to her and take her to the hospital.

"You haven't got any dead bodies in there, have you," asked Jimmy, "because she's frightened enough already without having to ride with some of those!"

Jimmy beamed back to where the young woman was lying, and she was doing fine, under the circumstances.

"Thank you for your help, Mr James," she said.

"Oh, it's all in a day's work for me, Claire," replied Jimmy, "you just take it easy and the ambulance will be here in a minute to get you to the hospital. I think you've been very lucky there my girl, and very brave, but everything looks fine now."

"It is, thanks to you Mr James," she said, "and I'm going to call him 'James' after you too. Peter James, because Peter is my husband's name. Do you mind if I call him after you?"

"Not at all lass," said Jimmy, "that's a nice name and he'll be proud of it one day, and you'll be proud of him, too."

She continued to talk to Jimmy while they waited for the ambulance. "I was going home from the city, back to Devon. We have a wonderful house, there. Little Peter James would have had an older brother, but he died in our swimming pool when he was three years old."

Jimmy looked carefully at her, and realised that this was Peter's wife, the one who was going to have the baby to replace little Mikey!

Before he could say anything else, there was a bright beam of light as a news team began to take some film of the scene. Camera rolling, the questions came by the bucket full.

Was your baby born in the wreckage?

Was your baby delivered by one of the paramedics?

What's your name?

What's the baby's name?

What's your name, Mr Paramedic?

Jimmy had seen the ambulance arrive and made his exit behind the news team.

Claire answered all of their questions and then was placed in the ambulance. The last thing she told them was that the paramedic, called Mr James, had delivered her baby. When the news team found out who she was, they said that they would contact Peter immediately, as they knew him from various places and reporting that they had done.

Peter got the phone call from his colleagues, and he went straight to the hospital to see his wife and their new son. The joy of knowing that she had survived a train crash *and* given birth to their child was overwhelming.

"Was it one of the doctors on the scene who helped you?" asked Peter.

"Oh no, it was a paramedic," she replied, "and he was so nice, it was like as if he were my father, helping me through it all. That's why I want to call him Peter after you, and James after him, if that's all right with you?"

"Of course it is," said Peter, "anything you want. And we owe this man a great debt of gratitude, I must find out who he was."

"You probably will," she said, "he will be on the news film tonight."

"Of course," said Peter, "and we can ring up the ambulance station and find out his name, perhaps get him a right good commendation, too."

"Yes," said his wife, "I think he deserves something like that."

The news came on the television while Peter was still in the hospital, so they watched it together. He saw the paramedic kneeling down beside his wife, who was nursing their new son. It only showed a brief shot of the paramedic.

"I reckon I've seen that bloke before," said Peter casually, "he doesn't half remind me of someone, but I can't for the life of me think who it is!"

"He was *so* nice," said Claire, "I'd like him to be one of the godparents for our new son. What do think?"

"Great idea," agreed Peter, "and we can have Gerry and Marie as well."

"Oh yes, our dearest friends who have been with us through so much heartache," said Claire.

"I've got to ring Gerry, that chap's face is really bothering me, I wonder if it's someone he might know," said Peter. "Back in a minute, babe."

Peter went off to find a telephone and called Gerry at work in the studios at Nottingham.

The telephone conversation between the two friends was just like their usual ones, as Peter often rang Gerry and asked if he'd seen some person on another station's news bulletin, and then they would check it out. Sometimes, if the other station had got something before they had, they would try and find the place and go straight there to get in on the action!

Peter:
Hello, Gerry?
Gerry:
Hi, is that you Peter?
Peter:
Yes, how are you up there in the cold north?
Gerry:
It's always warm where I am, these days. No more cold, outside filming for me, and for you too if the truth be known. How's life in the big city these days?
Peter:
Gerry, something really wonderful has just happened, and Checkers and his crew have screened it on the 6 o'clock slot. It was a train crash just south of London,
Gerry:
Oh, I didn't see that, but I'll get a view sent to me by their station, and watch it over the Internet link. What's happened, anyway?
Peter:
Claire was on the train that hit another train, head-on, and there were over a hundred people, commuters, killed. She was dragged from the wreckage by a paramedic who, believe it or not, delivered our new baby right at the side of the track!
Gerry:
Peter that's great! Are they both all right?

Peter:

Fine, yes, fine. She is in St Mary's right now, but the doctor reckons that whoever delivered our baby certainly knew what he was doing.

Gerry:

Did you find out who he was? Whoever he is, he deserves some kind of commendation, don't you think?

Peter:

You can't get a good look at him on the film, but I suppose the ambulance control will recognise him. Mind you, I bet they already know about this by now. It's strange, but I got the feeling that I've seen the man before, and I can't for the life of me think where it was.

Gerry:

I'll watch the news clip and ring you back. I usually remember faces that I've been connected with at some time. Have you got your mobile with you?

Peter:

Yes, but you can't have them switched on in the hospital.

Gerry:

Doesn't matter, I'll ring you later at home, all right mate?

Peter:

Fine. Catch up with you later, bye for now.

Gerry:

Cheers, mate.

Gerry rang the station and asked them to send him the footage, so that that they could use it for covering the story in the northern region. This was common practice amongst the news teams.

Gerry watched the clip and saw the train crash and people milling about, fire crews and police, railway engineers all trying to free people from the wreckage. Then came a little special report on a young mother, who was saved from the wreckage by a paramedic, who also delivered her baby at the side of the tracks. Gerry could only catch a fleeting glimpse of the man, as Peter had said, but he did look familiar to him. He sent the clip on to the newsroom, but asked one of the engineers to take a look at that part, and see if they could take out the face of the man.

"What, not another one of these," said the engineer, "like the man at the party?"

Gerry thought for a moment. It can't be, it was just his mind running rings around his thoughts. No, it was just a matter of seeing who this paramedic was.

The next day, when Gerry returned from lunch there was an envelope on his desk. It was from the engineer, who had taken a picture of the man's face and tried to get the best quality that allowed you to see who it was. Gerry slid his hand inside the envelope and pulled out the picture. His face went ashen and he dropped down into his chair in disbelief.

"It can't be!" he said to himself. "How on earth has he managed that?"

It was just about possible to recognise the face of Jimmy in the picture, complete with paramedic's jump-type suit and first aid kit.

He phoned Marie at home, Martin at the bank, who phoned their mother. Then he phoned Peter.

"Hi Peter. It's Gerry. You're not going to believe this so I'll tell you slowly."

"You mean that your father who is dead, is now a paramedic? He delivered our new baby?"

The whole family were astonished at this latest revelation of the "beyond the grave" actions of their father, but no one could understand fully what was happening, except, Hazel. 'And she pondered these things in her heart, all what the angel had said'.

CHAPTER ELEVEN

Travel Broadens the Mind

Andrew took Jimmy to one side and said to him, in a joking kind of way, "Jimmy, your conduct is faultless and you are to be commended for your handling of the track side birth, but you must stop getting yourself filmed and photographed. You are supposed to be Death, not Mr Good Body."

"Can't help it Andrew, it's just me, I can't get out of what I used to be like," said Jimmy.

"That's because you were always a good man, my friend," said Andrew, with his arm around his shoulder.

"Hang on a minute," said Jimmy, "when people put their arm around you and call you 'their good friend' it means they want something awful doing, doesn't it Andrew, matey? And what about that Samson bloke, where did you dig him up from? Scared the shhh ... crap out of me."

"He was a fine man in the Old Testament days, very strong, very powerful arms. At his last performance he really brought the house down."

"I noticed," snapped Jimmy.

"No, it's nothing for you to worry about this time, in fact, it's quite a treat for you," replied Andrew.

"Treat?" said Jimmy.

"Yes, treat", said Andrew. "*We* have been summoned, and now you will meet Gabriel and his gates, and ..."

"Him?" said Jimmy. "Why, what have you done wrong, Andrew? Don't worry, I'll stand up for you in court."

"We haven't done anything *wrong*," said Andrew. "It's more like, what we've done *right*! The handling of various situations with care and compassion has reached the ears of everyone, and I think you're going to get your reward at last!"

"Reward?" said Jimmy, "what reward?"

"Don't know for sure, mate, but I reckon you might be staying up in the 'top' quarters from now on, lucky you!" said Andrew, beaming with delight at his friend's forthcoming fortune.

"What, no more jobs, just take it easy and like the old song says," asked Jimmy, "that lucky old sun, has nothing to do, but roll around heaven all day."

"That's about it," said Andrew, "and you deserve it all, the pleasures and the glory, meeting old pals, old relatives that you haven't seen for many years!"

"Sounds thrilling," muttered Jimmy. "Anyway, I thought that we agreed on 'one day' when I first came up here?"

"It's over for you really, you've done more than you needed to and have earned this great reward," replied Andrew, "great isn't it?"

"So this is one way that people can earn their 'reward' so to speak," said Jimmy, "but what if they don't want to change their current status, what if they're quite happy doing what they're doing, what then?"

"I don't know, it's never happened like that before to my reckoning," replied Andrew, rubbing his head, "everybody always wants to get to the other place as quick as they can like as if it's the ultimate goal. I suppose He will make whatever changes to the rules as He wants."

Andrew asked Jimmy if he was ready, to which Jimmy nodded and they both were translated to the next place, just outside the most spectacular gates you ever saw!

"I've often wondered what these gates would actually look like," said Jimmy, "but this is beyond my wildest imagination!"

"You see," said Andrew, "things on the other side are so marvellous that the people on the earth plane wouldn't be able to take it in, until they have had their minds changed by actually crossing over."

"Dying!" chipped in Jimmy.

"Well, yes, I suppose you could say it like that," returned Andrew, "but we prefer the term 'crossing over' because that's really what it is, you came over to me and yet your spirit didn't die, did it?"

"No, just my body!" replied Jimmy.

"Yes, but that is because it was of no earthly use to you any more, pardon the pun," said Andrew, with a grin.

"I wish you wouldn't keep having these 'puns' all the time, you're starting to get me at it too!" said Jimmy.

Just then, a man appeared from inside the gates, and came towards them.

He looked to be about thirty years old, very strongly built, with long blonde hair and a kind face. His eyes were glowing with delight and he had a welcoming smile on his face.

"Andrew," he said in a very sweet voice, "you have brought Jimmy to us at last. We've been hearing all the news about your exploits, and we are all very keen to meet you."

Andrew turned to Jimmy, "Jimmy, meet Gabriel. Gabriel, this is Jimmy Coney."

Jimmy just stood there, frozen to the spot. "What do I address him as, Andrew, Saint or Angel, or what?"

Before Andrew could reply, Gabriel chipped in. "Jimmy, you can call me Gabriel, because here there are no titles for people who have crossed over. The only titles around here are as follows. God, Himself, you can call him Lord or your God. Then there are angels who are called by their own separate names. Cherubs have no names, as they are only called cherubs. The Seraphim are angels of a kind but they are normally in the presence of God Himself, so you might not see much of them."

"Any more questions?" asked Andrew.

"That'll be enough for now," replied Jimmy. "Anyway, Gabriel, what did you think when it was your time to cross over, were you ready?"

"Jimmy," said Andrew, "it's not really the thing to ask someone ..."

"No, it's all right," said Gabriel, "he's every right to be curious. I have always been here from the very beginning, and I can't remember being anything else or anywhere else. I was created here. I have been God's right-hand man, so to speak, for the eternity of time. I was here when the other angels began to make war against the heavenly host, and they were cast down to another level."

"Wow!" exclaimed Jimmy, "how come they wanted to make trouble in a place as beautiful as this?"

"You're always wanting to hear the fighting stories, aren't you?" said Andrew.

"It's alright, really," said Gabriel, and he touched Jimmy's forehead to install the full history of the heavenly war.

"Bloo ... Wow, I mean ...!" spluttered Jimmy.

"What did God think about that, then?" asked Jimmy, totally submerged in all this new knowledge, "I mean, wanting to cause ..."

Andrew tried to shut him up again, and Gabriel just smiled at his enthusiasm for knowledge.

Gabriel continued with a confident smile on his face.

"Anyway, we must press on, and show you around the Celestial City, now that you're here to stay. You really have earned your reward, Jimmy, and I'm pleased to meet you and show you to your mansion."

"This is where I will leave you now, Jimmy," said Andrew, "it really has been good working with you, and I hope your replacement will do just as well as you have. Don't forget to come back and see me sometime, will you?"

"Hold on a minute!" said Jimmy. "Is this all finalised then, don't I have a choice or anything to say on the matter?"

"What do you mean?" asked Gabriel. "Don't you want to live in the Celestial City?"

"Well, it's not that I don't want to live in the City, or live with you Gabriel, and probably the other celebrities, and listen to all their stories of Gabriel, but I just enjoy doing what I'm doing!"

Gabriel looked at Jimmy. "You are a strange fellow. Everyone I meet wants nothing else than to enter into the Celestial City, and here's you wanting to stay 'working' as you might say."

"Oh it's nothing to do with you lot and what have you," said Jimmy, "it's just that, I feel good, no, useful, doing what I do, helping people to cross over without getting lost or frightened. If I could have had this job on the earth plane instead of fixing gas pipes, I would have preferred it any day!"

"You can still have the tour of the city," said Gabriel, "you never know, it might just make you change your mind when we meet some of the other 'Celebs'. I'll tell God what you have said and we will see what He wants you to do. Don't forget, it's HIS will not ours."

"I would like that," said Jimmy, "I want to see the city that I have always been told about in church, and now I have met Gabriel face to face, but I don't know if I would want to stay there, yet."

They did the tour. In a twinkling of an eye! Back at the gates there was a beautiful mansion where Gabriel lived, where they met.

"Do you know, Gabriel," said Jimmy, "I feel like I have met you before somewhere, but that can't be possible, can it?"

"Well," replied Gabriel, "what about your spectacular dinner at the house of that young couple?"

"You, you were there?" stuttered Jimmy.

"Who do you think the other waiter was?" said Gabriel, "I enjoyed every minute of it, though you were a bit pushy when you were giving the orders, weren't you?"

"I'm so sorry, I didn't know you were …"

"Doesn't matter, we both had a good time!" said Gabriel. "Now, about you not wanting to come and live here, and stop working. God has given me the instruction to let you carry on doing your job and He is very pleased with you."

"Well," said Jimmy, after the initial shock of talking with Gabriel face to face, "I would like to continue with what I am doing, if that's all right with everybody!"

"Hmm," said Gabriel, "you are such a good man, and I think that you are doing something that needs to be done just the way that you are doing it. Don't change a thing, except you can have some more special powers to use for the good of the people you meet up with, instead of just being Mr Death all the time. That way, you can do some good around the world."

Jimmy smiled, enriched by the presence of Gabriel Himself, and thrilled at being allowed to carry on working as he was. He was also allowed automatic entry into the city whenever he wanted, so that he could come up and visit.

Gabriel touched his hand and bade him farewell and walked away. Jimmy felt like he had been electrocuted, and still lived. He felt his head tingle, right down through his legs. Then in a flash he was back with Andrew.

"Phew!" said Jimmy, "that was some meeting, mate!"

"You're back then?" replied Andrew with a grin.

"You betcha!" said Jimmy, gladly, "and what's on the horizon today my friend?"

"Well, you should see what I got out of it, first," replied Andrew, as he waved his hand across the large white screen in front of him. It cleared to show something in the region of two thousand people, standing in lines of probably a hundred each.

"What's all this then, Andrew?" asked Jimmy.

"These are my new helpers, controllers, processors you might say," said Andrew, like someone who had just received the best gift in the world, "and they are now processing more people than I could manage on my own."

"Go on then, numerate me!" said Jimmy in fun.

"Numbers?" replied Andrew, "Well I could only process something like a hundred thousand souls at a time, the rest had to be sent to a waiting area. Now I can get everyone processed as soon as they appear, no waiting! And, it looks like I can have more time off to jaunt around and go and see people."

"That's going to be interesting for you then, where to first?" said Jimmy.

While he was speaking, Andrew changed his appearance and became dressed in khaki shorts and a very loud, patterned shirt. Oh, and sandals!

Jimmy looked astonished, especially as Andrew had also changed his suit for something like the same, except he was wearing white trainers!

"What's all this then?" asked Jimmy.

"We are off to Miami for a spot of sun bathing," replied Andrew, and they were there! Walking on the fine sandy beach, with the waves rolling in, and steering round the many people sun bathing on the beach.

"This is absolutely brilliant!" shouted Jimmy, "I've only seen this in travel magazines."

"I've always dreamed of coming here, Jimmy," said Andrew, "but never had the time to do it. I told you in the beginning that you could go anywhere you wanted, and all you did was stay in Britain for some reason."

"I never thought about coming to America," said Jimmy, "fancy an ice cream?"

"Certainly," replied Andrew, "and a big glass of cool beer, how about you?"

"Certainly," said Jimmy, as they made their way to a beachside bar.

Another man joined them at the bar and sat on a stool at the side of Andrew.

"Hi there, buddy, hot for this time of year aint it?" the man said in a clearly American accent.

"Well, I wouldn't know really," replied Andrew, "this is our first time, here, we've only just arrived, Dan."

"You know this man?" chipped in Jimmy, "Out of all the people on the beach, the first person to speak to you is someone you know?"

Dan smiled across at Jimmy, "Of course he knows me, I'm one of you, Jimmy, and I've heard all about your spectacular antics in good old England, too. Where did you learn all the theatrical stuff for the dinner, and how about delivering a baby! I couldn't have done all that, I just get 'em and send 'em in to Andrew."

"Well, it's just how it works out sometimes," replied Jimmy in a modest sort of way.

"Anyway, Jimmy, I'm Dan De'Ath, and how about you come and work with me for a while to give me some pointers?"

"What, in America?" asked Jimmy.

"Doesn't matter where you are," said Andrew, "you can deliver souls from anywhere that I send you, just that you always seem to want to play at home. Anyway, didn't you once tell your wife that 'travel broadens the mind' when you got her off on that first holiday?"

"Well, yes I did, but that was when I was *alive* wasn't it!" replied Jimmy.

Dan and Andrew laughed. The trio sat and baked in the sun, sipping ice-cold beer and licking on large cones of ice cream.

"Is this *really* what it's like being dead?" said Jimmy, quietly.

"Not for everyone, some just want to stay on their next level and enjoy all the new things," said Andrew. Dan agreed.

"It would be good for you to have a few experiences in another country, Jimmy," said Andrew, "how about working with Dan for a . . ."

"Not a *day* again?" chipped in Jimmy, quickly, "you got me with that one before!"

"He signed you up for a whole *day*!" said Dan, "that's a heck of a long time!"

"I know *now*," said Jimmy, "but I was a bit new to the surroundings before! You know, 'new kid on the block' as they say."

"We don't talk in days anymore though, do we Jimmy?" asked Andrew.

"No, we're good mates now, aren't we?" said Jimmy.

Andrew just smiled and sipped and licked, and the other two joined him.

When they had been there for a few hours, Andrew announced that it was time for him to go back, but gave each of them two names and locations to go to, in America.

Jimmy shook hands with Dan and made an instant partnership. Dan would show him around and Jimmy would have a go at doing his job in America.

They beamed themselves over to a busy street in Los Angeles that was full of cars, cabs and people, more than Jimmy had never seen before in his life.

"Spirit or body mode, Jimbo, what do you normally do?" asked Dan.

"I think spirit mode would be best to get through this lot," replied Jimmy, as they both moved slowly along the sidewalk (pavement) of the busy street. On arrival at their first address, they changed into body mode and into sharp suits with white shirts and ties. It was a huge office block, a skyscraper of something like eighty storeys high. Jimmy looked up and could only just make out the top floor as it disappeared into the clouds.

"Wow!" he said, "this is something else!"

Dan smiled, "You'll get used to this sort of thing in America, everything's bigger!"

"Are we going in then?" asked Jimbo, (Jimmy) "and who are we looking for today?"

"Guy on the thirteenth floor, named Harry Cropper, he's going to snort some drug up his nose and it's uncut. This will be his last 'trip' pardon my pun, Jimbo," replied Dan.

"Not you as well!" sighed Jimmy.

"How do you mean buddy?" said Dan.

"Where did you get that saying from, 'pardon the pun'," said Jimmy, "and I'll bet you don't know, do you?"

"I never used to say anything like that when I was alive, and driving those big trucks that you see, it's just something that I've heard recently, I guess," replied Dan.

"I'll tell you where it comes from, shall I?" said Jimmy in fun, "that little baldy man with the shiny head and smooth voice, Andy baby! He says it all the time, and he's got me started with it too!"

They both had a laugh and made a serious pact to try and *not* say that phrase again!

They entered the building, and were immediately greeted by a security man wearing a brown uniform and hat. And he carried a gun. Jimmy didn't know that over there they could carry guns, as he had never been to America before. Anyway, that didn't bother him so much, now. He looked very impressive to say the least, as he asked for their passes and nature of their business.

Jimmy took the lead before Dan could say anything. "We have some private business with Mr Cropper on the thirteenth, and we don't want to be late," said Jimmy, as he smiled his English smile and blew gently on the security man's face.

The man turned and sat down again at his desk, wiping a little sweat from his brow, and wondering to himself whether he was coming down with something.

Dan looked at Jimmy, and Jimmy at Dan.

"Beam us up to thirteenth then, Mr De'Ath," said Dan.

"Right away, Mr De'Ath," replied Jimmy, and they were there.

As they walked into the office, through the door, this time, they looked around for their client, but couldn't see him straight away.

Dan tapped the shoulder of Jimmy and said, "He's in the bathroom."

"Bathroom?" said Jimmy, "do they have bathrooms in their offices in America?"

"No, not a room with a bath tub in it, it's our name for the room where you can go and take a leak," replied Dan.

"Oh, a toilet?" said Jimmy, "why don't you just call it a toilet, then?"

"Right, a toilet. The bathroom is a toilet. Let's get in there," replied Dan, as he hurried Jimmy along.

They opened the door so as not to scare anyone else that might be in there, to find Harry Cropper leaning over the sink and preparing his drug. Some time ago he had become really stressed with his work at the office, and then his wife left him and went to live with someone else. He got onto heroin then, which helped, but found that once he was on it, he was hooked for life.

"How do you want to play this one, Jimbo?" asked Dan. "Any ideas to make it more interesting before we sting him?"

"Sting him?" asked Jimmy, "what's all this 'sting him' business? We're here to help the man make the transition to the processing level, and we must make it as smooth as possible for him."

Jimmy smiled at Dan, and the comedy of what Jimmy had said in his perfect English accent, like the actor James Mason, was seen by both of them.

"Mr Harry Cropper?" asked Jimmy.

"Who wants to know?" replied Cropper. "If you're from the frigging I.R.S. or you are my frigging wife's solicitor you can go and get …"

"No, no!" interrupted Jimmy, "we are here to try and help you through a difficult situation that you seemed to have got yourself into. The drugs!"

Cropper looked at them both, with a disbelieving sneer and said, "Just who the frigging hell are you two guys, before I call security and have you thrown out?"

Before Dan could answer, the security man from the lobby walked into the washroom.

"Hey, you!" snapped Cropper to the security guard, "throw these two frigging assholes out and don't let them back in again, do you hear?"

The guard looked at Cropper with amazement, "What two assholes, Mr Cropper?"

"These two frigging morons stood here beside me!" replied Cropper, "Are you frigging blind or what?"

"Mr Cropper," said the guard, "there is no one else in here only you and me. Are you sure you're all right?"

Cropper looked at the guard, and then at Jimmy and Dan, who smiled politely back at him. Then Jimmy walked forward towards the guard and passed straight through him.

He turned, and smiled again at Cropper, who by this time was wide-eyed and open mouthed.

"Everything all right Mr Cropper?" asked the guard.

"Yeah, yeah, I'm fine, just get out of here and leave me alone!" replied Cropper.

The guard left, giving Cropper a cautious look as he passed by him.

"The guard has it in his mind to get someone up here to take a look at you," said Dan to Cropper, "and when he comes back ..."

"And when he comes back I'll have taken this shit and will be my old charming self again," snapped Cropper, "and they'll think *he's* the frigging asshole then, won't they?"

"Mr Cropper, Harry old chap," began Jimmy, "we have been sent here to take you across to the other side, when you die. We mean you no harm, and we can wait till you're ready. You see, that stuff that you are about to sniff up your nose is uncut, crude, and it's the last trip you will be going on, pardon the pun, apart from the one that you are going on with us."

"What's all this shit!" snarled Cropper, "and have less of the 'Harry' bit too, you aint no friend of mine to call me Harry. Now get out of here while I freshen up."

"Take that and you really will come a cropper," said Jimmy.

"Pardon the pun," added Dan, and they looked at each other with a grin, "I had to get that in, buddy, and you left yourself wide open!"

While they were having their fun, Cropper took a large sniff at the stuff in the little tin foil ashtray on the cabinet, in front of the mirror. As he did, he looked into the mirror and couldn't see the two men standing behind him.

Thinking that they had gone, he turned to wipe his hands, and saw that they were still standing behind him. He looked straight into the mirror again, then behind him. They didn't have a reflection!

"Hey, what's all this shhh . . .?"

Before he could finish what he was about to say, he collapsed onto the floor. His spirit stood up beside Jimmy and Dan.

"What's happened to me?" shouted Cropper, "how come I'm standing here with you two frigging moron ghosts, and yet I'm laid there on the floor?"

"You're about to die," announced Dan, calmly.

"Die! Die? Me, die?" screamed Cropper, "I'm going to call someone to get help, I'm not going to let you two frigging morons get away with this shit!"

Dan had to have another little laugh at Cropper's expense, "Who ya gonna call? Ghostbusters?"

Jimmy burst out laughing and the two of them made quite a joke out of it, repeating it two or three more times. Cropper stood there amazed at their hilarity, when he was in such a desperate situation.

"Hey, you two assholes, what's so funny," snapped Cropper, "you wait till I get some help in here!"

Just then the guard appeared through the door, accompanied by two more men. They rushed to the body and turned him over, testing for a pulse in the neck.

"There, see, they've found me!" snarled Cropper, "now you two can get lost because I'm going nowhere, they'll have me back on my feet in no time. I've been like this before after a snort."

Dan and Jimmy looked at him and shook their heads.

"Cropper, you're time is now, they can't revive you, you're already dead," said Dan in a friendly, caring voice.

"You just frigging wait, moron, they've already called for the paramedics!" snarled Cropper.

The paramedics arrived in minutes, and began to check for a pulse. No pulse could be found. They tried heart massage and finally the electric shock. The first two attempts on low power proved useless.

"Bang it on full power!" shouted Cropper as he watched with great concern.

Just as if the paramedics had heard him, they used full power and there was nothing.

"We're getting nowhere here," announced one of the men, "let's call it in and get the Coroner's wagon round here straight away."

"You can't just leave me like this!" screamed Cropper.

The guard stood by the body to watch over it until the police and the coroner arrived. Cropper looked on with concern, and then said in his abusive manner, "You frigging morons have set all this up, haven't you? Who the frigging hell are you two, anyway?"

"We told you," said Dan, "we have come to take you over to the other side, you know, like you watch on television, John Edward?"

"Yeah, I've seen that John Edward guy on the television talking to dead spirits, or supposed to be!" snarled Cropper. "Bet he can just pretend and still get a big bung for acting like an asshole, can't he?"

"He doesn't pretend, Harry," said Jimmy, "he really does communicate with the other side, where we come from. That's where you're going to now, and we are going to make a better person out of you, too."

"I don't think so, asshole number frigging one, I'm staying right here till they get me back into my body," growled Cropper.

Dan looked up to the ceiling and said, "Andrew, beam us up for processing," and the three of them disappeared.

Andrew dealt with Cropper and did the re-training session, and yes, he was a better person, or spirit.

As Dan and Jimmy were about to move on to their next job, Cropper came back with Andrew.

"Hey you guys," he said in a quiet voice, "I really want to say how sorry I am for being such an as ..."

"Careful," said Andrew, "remember where you are!"

"Sorry Mr Andrews," said Cropper, " I just want to tell these guys how sorry I am. You see, I haven't had such a good life since everything went wrong, and I guess it does create a nasty person out of anyone, do you know what I mean?"

"Of course we do, buddy," said Dan, "but you will be all right now, and you can find all the answers from up here, set your mind at rest."

"Answers," said Cropper, "like who did my wife run off with, who spiked the heroin and in fact, murdered me! What did my best friend say when they told him that I was deceased!"

"Yes, all of those questions," said Jimmy, "in fact, we'll help you, won't we, Dan?"

"Sure thing, Jimbo," replied Dan, "let's take him back in time for the ride of his life! Pardon the pun."

"Right," agreed Jimmy, "let's go!"

The three of them disappeared from Andrew's side and were back in the bathroom (toilet) at the office where Harry Cropper had died. His body was still on the floor with the guard standing watch over it, when in came Harry's best friend, Glen Schafer.

"Hey, that's Schafer!" exclaimed Harry, "he's my best friend and colleague. I've known him for twenty years. He's gonna be really upset at seeing me lying there, dead."

Schafer looked at the body. "You bloody asshole," he said, "this is just what you deserved, especially after what you did to your wife, Anna, who is now living with me! She did right to leave a loser like you, you asshole, druggie, and garbage of a man! No, not a man, just a friggin asshole!"

Harry stood and listened, open-mouthed. He couldn't believe his ears or his eyes!

"He was my best mate," said Harry, "and he took my wife! I didn't know that she went to live with him, he never said anything about that in four years!"

The guard left the scene for a moment to see who was outside the door. It was the police and the Coroner. While he was gone, Glen shared another secret with his unknown audience.

"I hope you liked your last blast! Friggin asshole! That will teach you! I got that one especially for you from a friend of mine, called Anna. I hope you rot in hell, you fat slob of a bastard!"

"You see," said Dan, "you never really know who your friends are, do you?"

"That's true," agreed Harry, "but to think that he never really cared about me, and thought such bad things of me, yet worked alongside me like a brother!"

"Not to worry," said Jimmy, "just too bad that you had to wait till you were dead to find these things out. And the worst thing is, he will get away with your murder because everyone thinks that he is your best friend. And that you just bought some bad heroin!"

"I would never have thought it!" said Harry. "What happens now, mates?"

"You're going back upstairs and we're off to do another job" said Dan. "Come on Jimbo, let's hit the road."

"Right oh, Daniel," replied Jimmy, "we'll catch up with you later, Harry."

The three of them left the scene in the capable hands of the Coroner's assistant, and the police. Probably this was the perfect murder.

Dan and Jimmy went to the next location, which happened to be a diner on the outskirts of Jacksonville. This was a favourite stop for truckers and van drivers, as well as tourists from all over the world. Dan was a little upset with this one, as it was a trucker who was next in the frame for crossing over, and he used to be a trucker.

"A bit close to the bone?" asked Jimmy. "Do you want me to take this one and you can catch up with me later?"

"You might say, Jimbo," replied Dan, "but we all have to do what we have to do. No, no, I'll be fine."

"How did you cross over, anyway?" asked Jimmy, "you never did tell me."

"You never asked," said Dan, with a little grin and a hint of lightness coming into his voice again. "It was like this, Jimbo. I used to drive these big, big trucks for something like twelve hours every day of the week. Saturday and Sunday were my days off, but I would work them too if they wanted a load taking somewhere. I was crazy about trucks and the whole thing about being a trucker, the lifestyle, everything. I never got married, I wasn't in one place long enough to meet a girl and settle down. I suppose, being on my own for such a long time each day, you get used to it. I must admit though, I would have liked to have settled down with a good woman and had a family. One day I'm hurtling down the road and I got this big pain across my stomach."

"Appendicitis?" chipped in Jimmy.

"No, hunger," came back Dan. "I spotted a diner in the distance and planned to pull over, even get a bed for the night. I pulled in and parked the truck, and as I was getting out of the cab, two guys with woolly hats on, jumped me from behind. A third guy started punching into my big empty stomach."

"Did they kill you?" asked Jimmy with great interest.

"No, well, not at first. I grabbed the two guys who were holding me from behind, and banged them together. Then I picked up the third guy and threw him through the air into the side of another truck, and he didn't get up anymore. Then I saw another guy come from behind the front of the truck, holding out a gun in front of him. I started towards him and heard this big bang. I guess he must have shot me in the head, because that's all I remember. Andrew filled me in later, like we did with poor old Harry. And that's how come I do this now for a living, pardon the pun."

"Did they get your cargo, was it something valuable?" asked Jimmy.

"Sure did," said Dan with a grin, "twenty four tons of corn flakes!"

They had a laugh and then decided that it was time to carry on.

"What's the low-down with this client then, Dan?" asked Jimmy.

"I think Andrew said it was an accident just down the road, so we'd better get fixed up with a ride," replied Dan.

"A ride," asked Jimmy, "what, a horse each?"

"Nah, Jimbo, your sense of humour can be cruel at times, just like mine, but I love it!" replied Dan. "We will have a car when the time comes, but we'll have to go inside and make sure that our 'sting' is in the joint first. He may not have got here yet."

"I can't get that word, Dan, 'sting', it sounds awful, as if we are going to electrocute him or poke him to death with a pointed stick."

"Oh I know, it's just a bit of slang that I heard in some film, and it sometimes comes out without me thinking of what I'm saying," said Dan. "Anyway, what do you call it, Jimbo?"

"Well, I think the proper name is something like 'crosser' or 'esgotcha' which I think is not as good as 'client', which is what I usually call them," replied Jimmy.

"How's that one again, 'esgotcha' is that?" asked Dan.

"That's right," said Jimmy, "you're supposed to go up to your client and shout, 'es got cha' and then grab them."

Dan couldn't stop laughing at such a silly joke, and he fell straight in for it.

"This English humour is going to be the death of me, pardon the pun," groaned Dan as he carried on with a bellyaching laugh. Then they both laughed at what Dan had just said. "The death of me!" repeated Dan a couple of times.

Eventually they pulled themselves together and got back to what they were supposed to be doing, as a large truck pulled onto the parking lot in front of the diner. It was their client, a medium built man in his thirties, quite handsome, and definitely a ladies' man. Dan and Jimmy followed him into the diner, where he sat at a window seat and ordered coffee and breakfast.

Dan and Jimmy sat in the seat behind him, so that they could monitor what went off next, to see if they could get any clues as to the nature of his forthcoming accident. As they listened and drank their coffee, it became apparent that he was meeting one of the waitresses who worked there. Although he was married to a girl in another town, he could never resist a pretty face.

Sure enough, the waitress came and sat down at his table. She looked distressed and began to blurt out all the misery that her husband was causing her at home. How he was always beating her and suspecting her of carrying on with other men. How right he was too! Eventually, the truck driver calmed her down with his arm around her shoulder and lots of little kisses on her face, then a long kiss on her lips. Dan was so taken up with listening, that he didn't realise that he was staring!

The trucker looked up and caught sight of Dan's gaze.

"What the hell are you looking at, bastard?" snarled the trucker.

"Sorry buddy," answered Dan in a very mild manner, "I guess I was far away in my thoughts, I wasn't looking at you."

"Oh yes you were!" the trucker snarled back again. "What's up, do you want some of her too?"

"No, no, buddy, she's, er, all yours, sorry," replied Dan.

"You're very restrained," said Jimmy quietly, "don't you fancy a little bit of 'fisticuffs' today, Daniel?"

"Quiet, we mustn't get involved, and if I did hit him he would land up at the side of Andrew!" replied Dan.

It was too late, the trucker had already decided that he must show off his manly attitude to his girlfriend, and defend her reputation. He got up from his seat and called out Dan for a fight.

Dan didn't know what to do at first, so he just got up and turned, moving into the aisle. The trucker took a shot at him with his right fist, and Dan just caught hold of it. Then, as Dan released his grip, the trucker tried for a shot at Dan's chin with his left fist. Dan caught hold of that too. Then Dan put out his hand to give the trucker a handshake, but instead, the trucker tried another blow to Dan's face. Dan didn't stop him this time and the blow fell flat with a deadening thud on Dan's cheek.

"God! I think I've broken my hand!" screamed the trucker. "Don't just stand there, get me some ice and a bandage!"

"Let me have a look at it," said Jimmy, calmly, "I used to be a first-aider some time ago when I was working."

The trucker held out his arm and hand for Jimmy to see. It was definitely a case of three broken fingers and a fractured wrist. Jimmy bound it up with a large bandage that another waitress had brought, and then looked at the place on Dan's cheek where it had connected.

"You'll be fine old boy," said Jimmy, "but make sure that you eat plenty of ice cream."

Dan looked at Jimmy and then couldn't help but burst into laughter. Jimmy chuckled along with Dan's boisterous laughter, but the trucker couldn't understand why they were having jokes when he was in so much pain.

"All right you two," he shouted, "tell me how I'm going to get to the hospital to have this looked at properly, and what about my truck?"

Dan looked at Jimmy, and Jimmy at Dan, waiting for each other to make some suggestion.

Jimmy took Dan to one side and whispered, "If he's supposed to have an accident down the road, I think we've just cocked up the whole plan."

"Suppose we have, really," replied Dan, "but what can we do?"

Just then they both looked around to see Andrew walk in through the door.

"We've had it now, Jimbo," said Dan, "here comes the boss."

Andrew smiled at them both and said in his calm and collected way, "I leave you two together for five minutes and this is what you get up to. You're supposed to be guiding people over, not brawling in diners."

"Sorry boss," said Dan.

"Me too," added Jimmy, "but things just got out of hand when the trucker thought that Dan was eyeing his girlfriend."

"I know what happened," said Andrew, "and here's what you must do to put things back on track. Dan, you offer to drive the truck to the hospital and take 'Jimbo' with you. I'll take care of the rest of the details from there. Can you manage that?"

"Sure thing, Andy Baby," said Dan, "leave it to us."

"I don't particularly like the name 'Andy' or Baby', Mr De'Ath, but get on with your assignment."

Andrew sat down and ordered a cup of English tea and some toasted muffins, while Dan and Jimmy went back over to the trucker.

"O.K. buddy," said Dan, "we've worked out a plan to get you out of trouble. It's this. I will drive you and your truck to the hospital and get you all fixed up, then we'll see what needs doing from there."

"That's fine by me," said the trucker, "but I don't want any funny business with you two!"

"We are very sorry for what has happened," said Jimmy, "and after all, it's now down to us to get you sorted out."

The three of them left the diner and went to the truck, while Andrew smiled at them through the window, sipping his tea. Dan helped Jimmy to get up inside, and then the trucker. Then he climbed up into the driver's seat and started up the big truck.

"This brings back memories, Jimbo," said Dan with a big grin on his face, "hold onto your hats!"

He drove off from the diner and shifted through the multiple gears of the truck with ease, impressing both his passengers, and getting up to the fifty-five miles per hour speed limit in no time. The nearest hospital was five miles away, and the drive took very little time. At the hospital the trucker received attention from a nurse, who suspected a broken wrist and three fingers, just like Jimmy had said, back at the diner. Dan and Jimmy waited around whilst the trucker had some x-rays and was bandaged properly. He came out to where the two were waiting and told them that he had to get his truck back to a depot, thirty miles away, but couldn't drive.

"No problem, buddy," said Dan, "we'll take you there, truck and all. Then we will find our own way back."

"That's mighty nice of you guys," said the trucker, "and hey, I'm sorry about the fight and all that at the diner."

"No problem," said Dan, beaming one of his big smiles, "but I wasn't really looking at your lady, I was just staring into space."

"I usually have trouble from guys who make eyes at my dates," said the trucker, "suppose it comes with the territory, being out on the road and all that."

"When I was trucking, I didn't bother with the ladies, as I was always more interested in trucks!" said Dan. "Never could settle down either, got diesel in my blood."

They started off again for the depot, with Big Dan honking the air horns and singing some truck driving song that he could remember from way back.

"Dan," said Jimmy, "do we have to have all this? You're like a big kid with a new toy."

"Sorry Jimbo," replied Dan, "that's how we get through all those long and lonely miles."

He turned to the trucker and said, "By the way, I'm Dan and this is my buddy, Jimbo."

"I'm Dwight, Dwight Merville," replied the trucker.

"Merville," continued Dan, "hey that's something to do with aviation isn't it?"

"No relation though," answered Dwight, "otherwise I wouldn't be driving trucks for a living."

They took a left at an intersection, (junction) and headed for Dwight's depot. Dan noticed a car following them up close, and weaving about as if trying to pass or look into the driving mirror to see who was driving.

"Got anyone who might be bothered about your whereabouts, Dwight?" asked Dan.

Dwight looked into the other mirror and saw the car.

"No one that I know, wonder why they're acting so strange?" said Dwight.

A mile further on the car pulled alongside and the passenger wound the window down, shouting something like "pull over" and showing Dan some kind of official badge.

"Look's like the law," said Dan, as he started slowing up and changing down through the gears. He brought the truck to a stop in a lay-by and switched off the engine. The three of them got out and walked around to the front of the truck where the car had pulled in.

"Who are you, and what do you want?" shouted Dan.

The badge didn't come out again, instead, there was a gun. They weren't Law Officers, they had other business in mind.

One of the men spoke first. "We want that son of a bitch, he's been seeing my wife!"

Jimmy assumed that this was the girl that they had left behind at the diner, and his suspicions were confirmed when he noticed her sitting in the back of the car. She didn't seem bothered about Dwight, in fact, she seemed quite happy with the man that was waving the gun. This smacked of memories for Dan, a man pointing a gun at the front of his truck. Then he nudged Jimmy.

"I think this is Andrew's plan, so we'll just go along with what happens, yes?"

"Yes," replied Jimmy quietly, "it looks like that to me, too."

An argument ensued for a little while between Dwight and the two men, and then one of them called the girl from the car. She was to confirm that Dwight had led her on and tried to get her to run away with him. Dwight looked shocked at her words, but could not convince the men of anything different.

When he tried to tell them how she had come on to him each time he went to the diner, and how she had told him that her husband was always beating her, they wouldn't hear of it. It made the first man, the one with the gun, even angrier to hear that and he took aim at Dwight. Dwight shouted, "Don't be stupid!" but a shot rang out and he fell to the ground.

The two men looked at the body lying on the ground, then grabbed the girl and sped off in the car. Dan and Jimmy stood there for a moment until Dwight's spirit stood up beside them.

"Did you see that?" exclaimed Dwight. "They shot at me, and all over that dumb broad of a girl!"

He looked at Dan and Jimmy, and then at himself.

"What's happened to me?" he asked. "Why am I standing here with you, when my body is lying on the ground, there?"

"Dwight old buddy," said Dan, "I hate to have to explain this to you, but when that guy pulled the trigger he shot you."

"You mean ..."

"That's about it, buddy, you're dead," answered Dan.

"Then how come I'm still standing here talking with you guys," said Dwight, "shouldn't I be wearing wings and floating off into the sky if I'm dead. You're kidding with me, aren't you? Come on guys stop messing about. What are we going to do now?"

"We have actually been sent to help you to cross over, Dwight," said

Jimmy, "so that you don't go floating off into the unknown and get yourself lost."

"Who the hell are you then," asked Dwight.

"We are actually, I suppose you might say, the 'Angels of Death' that have come to take you across," replied Jimmy.

Dwight continued to argue the situation, "But what about all that back there at the diner, and driving the truck, and the fight and ..."

"Nearly all part of the plan to make your transition to the spirit world easier, although things did go a little different to plan," said Jimmy.

"So I'm dead, then," asked Dwight.

"Yep, 'fraid so buddy," said Dan, "and you're gonna have to come with us now, to the next level, to the big 'diner' in the sky."

A large, white, stretch limousine pulled into the lay-by, and the rear door opened as if to invite the three men to get in.

"This guy might be able to help me, bring me back to life!" said Dwight as they walked towards the open door.

Inside the luxurious motor sat Andrew, listening to some classical music. He smiled at them as they got in, and immediately they were at Andrew's place, and Dwight was processed.

Andrew gave them some more clients and sent them off, back to work with one comment, "Don't get into any more bother you two, just do the job, please."

CHAPTER TWELVE

Memories

After quite a long time in America, and many hundreds of clients processed with the help of Dan, Jimmy found himself wanting to visit his family again to see how things were developing.

"Is it normal for spirits to get homesick?" he asked.

"Yes, I suppose it is with some people," replied Andrew.

"Have you ever wanted to visit Sherwood Forest and your little inn, back in the days when Robin Hood was a customer?" asked Jimmy.

"No," came the quick reply, "it holds too many bad memories. After all, I did have to watch my wife and daughter killed before I was hacked to death by that wicked sheriff."

Andrew saw that Jimmy had been very busy and perhaps a little time off might not go amiss.

"Do you want to have some time off, Jimmy?" asked Andrew. "You can you know, if you want to."

"What would I do? Where would I go?" said Jimmy.

"Have a look around on the 'earth plane' and see what's happening with your family, take a trip to some far off place and soak up the atmosphere, the beach!" said Andrew.

"No fun on your own though, is it?" replied Jimmy. "When I was alive I did all those things with my wife, I had company."

"Go and visit her," suggested Andrew, "but don't get into anything – well, you know what I'm trying to say, don't you?"

"You mean trouble don't you?" said Jimmy.

"Well, not so much trouble, but, don't disturb the momentum of history, to put it bluntly," said Andrew, "and don't keep getting yourself photographed."

"I know what you mean, mate, and yes, it would be good to see how they're all doing," agreed Jimmy.

"See you in a couple of minutes, then?" said Andrew.

"See you in a couple of minutes, Andrew," said Jimmy, "and thanks."

"Don't mention it my friend," replied Andrew.

Jimmy beamed himself down to the little house where he used to live, and backtracked the moment to a couple or so years ago, just to remind himself of the fantastic memories that he had gained with Hazel. There was the new car on the drive. That brought back some more memories of the time when they went out to Afghanistan after Gerry and his friend.

Within the twinkling of an eye he was back there, in Kabul, at the hotel. He looked around the room and saw Hazel getting her coat on to leave. He went to the window and saw Marie arriving with that very big four-wheel drive monster of a jeep. She looked so perfect for the job, at least, now that he knew her capabilities!

"Oh Jimmy," he thought, "if only you had taken better care of yourself when you had the chance, you could still be alive for many more of these special memorable occasions."

He beamed up to the hospital in the mountains, and watched as the Taliban troops bombarded and machine-gunned every little piece of it. They shot nearly all the people that were there, only a few escaped by hiding in the scrub and bushes behind it. He saw Peter and Gerry, crouching in the bushes with some of the hospital staff, frightened for their lives. He moved closer in to within arm's length of Gerry, and smiled to himself.

"Come on Gerry, lad, you've been in worse scrapes than this, haven't you?" he thought.

Just as if Gerry had heard him, he said to Peter, "Can we get any messages out of here on anything?"

Peter looked at him and answered, "If we can link that field radio up to our satellite dish we might just be able to bridge the international phone lines to England."

"Got to be worth a try, hasn't it?" said Gerry.

"Who would we call?" asked Peter. "McGuire?"

"Not likely," snapped Peter, "he'd be no use at all, in fact, he would probably disown us anyway."

"Who then?" asked Peter again.

"Get in touch with my dad, he'll know what to do," said Gerry with some kind of confidence that made Peter feel confident too! "I feel as though he's watching over me right now, and I know that he'll find someone to help us."

Jimmy watched for a moment as they messed about with wires and batteries, and then cranked up the field telephone. He heard his own voice answer at the other end, and then beamed himself back to the little house in England. He remembered so clearly the events of that night, when all seemed lost, then it all took shape and happened. He first met Marie, and never for one minute imagined that she would become his daughter-in-law. He remembered the speech that he gave at his birthday-cum-engagement party, and meeting Marie's father for the first time. Burt. How many good nights did he and Hazel have with Burt and Linda, they were like brothers and sisters, all thinking the same way about everything. There was always time at each night out, especially when the drink had been flowing, for putting the world to right! "Ah, happy days and foggy nights," thought Jimmy.

Then he beamed into the house where Hazel was standing by the bed, talking to him. It was when he had just returned from the meeting with Sir Malcolm Hartley, at the television centre in Nottingham. Jimmy watched for a moment as Hazel gave him a hug and a kiss. Then he heard himself say, "Phew, it just felt like someone had walked over my grave, is it cold in here to you?"

Jimmy was a little startled as he remembered saying that, and now he knew why, because someone had virtually walked over, from his grave. Yes, it was himself!

He had felt something strange in the bedroom that night, but would never had realised then that the spirit that was visiting their house, was his own from the future.

This made Jimmy feel quite strange. He was looking at himself from the future, after he had died!

"I wonder," he thought, "how many spirits are passing about in this dimension, looking for people they know, looking for answers as to why they died suddenly, or even, why they died at all."

Then Jimmy beamed forward in time to the present day, standing in the lounge of his own house, nearly three years after he had died! Hazel came in from outside and busied about in the kitchen, and then came into the lounge to polish the furniture. She stopped working for a moment and looked around the room. She could sense that something was different in there today.

"Jimmy," she said quietly, "are you there my love?"

Jimmy looked on, and then blew a whisper of breath across her face, like the kiss of an angel.

"My Jimmy," said Hazel, "you'll never leave me, and I will always love you. Why can't you talk to me again?"

Jimmy didn't know whether to go into body mode or not.

"I suppose it won't hurt, once in a while," said Andrew, "but be careful not to change anything to do with her history or future."

"Thanks mate," said Jimmy, as he changed into a see-able body mode and said quietly, "Hazel, I'm here my love."

Hazel turned and saw him, tears began to stream, but she didn't know whether or not she could touch him.

Jimmy felt his arm, and then his leg, and then walked towards her and held out his hand.

"Have you come to take me with you? Am I going to die now?" said Hazel.

"No lass, It's only a flying visit to see if you're all right, and make sure that my family is fine," said Jimmy.

He held her hand and then embraced her for a moment. This was strange for a ghost to be able to do this, apart from the fact that Jimmy had earned some special privileges on account of his work. And he could change into a body mode that was see-able and touchable by other people. Whilst in this mode, he was also see-able by other spirits that were travelling about too, so he could have the best of both worlds.

Hazel told Jimmy about the two sons and their families, and all about how Burt and Linda *had* stayed friends with her, and been a real comfort to her. She told him that they still had good nights, and went to various places and functions together.

"By the way," said Hazel, "Marie is expecting your grandchild in six months, she has just announced her pregnancy last week."

Jimmy was overjoyed, and said that he would drop by and see the baby when it was born, almost as if he were still alive! He and Hazel chuckled about it, and she found herself talking to her deceased husband as naturally as though he were still alive. Then he bade her farewell, and said that he had to get back to work, but would come and see her again.

"Can you come and go as you please from up there, Jimmy?" asked Hazel.

"Well, it's like this, love," began Jimmy, "I am expected to be all over the place, just like when I was working on the pipes, here there and everywhere. Sometimes I get a couple of minutes to spare, so I come down and have a look around here. I have a special power of changing into spirit or body that I use in my job, so that makes it easy for me to go wherever I want. I've been to Miami Beach too! You ought to go to America it's a lovely place."

"Sounds like you're better off now than when you were alive Jimmy Coney!" said Hazel with a grin.

"It's not quite the same as being here with you and the family, which is something I'd give anything to have again," replied Jimmy, sadly. "That's something everyone ought to think about before doing anything silly like working themselves into the ground, drinking themselves to death, or smoking themselves into an early grave."

Jimmy kissed Hazel on the cheek and said goodbye, then beamed himself over to Martin's house. Martin was at work and Cath was doing her housework, and everything looked perfect.

Over at Gerry's house there was no one at home, so Jimmy beamed in on the place where Gerry was at that moment. It was the television centre where he worked, and he was having a meeting with some other technicians and people, to sort out the good news stories for the evening slot. There were several papers and pictures on the table, and each person had different thoughts on which was the prime story.

Jimmy looked through the pictures and saw one of Marie, which was on the bottom of the pile. She had been involved in some fund-raising scheme for children, but no one had taken the initiative to publicise it, and it was hard to get the money flowing in. Then, near to that was a picture of the countryside of Afghanistan, where the fighting was just about over. On top of these were something like thirty or forty other stories for consideration and it looked like someone had arranged them in their present order.

"OK," said Gerry at long last, "we've got to have something for the six o'clock slot which is topical and then something for the later slot which is humanistic."

As he leaned forward to pick up the photographs, Jimmy mixed them up so that the picture of Afghanistan was on the top, and the picture of Marie was next.

"I've sorted them out into some kind of order," said one of the men, "if you'd just like to take a look, Gerry. I thought we'd start off with the news of Malaysia and the . . ."

"But the first pictures are Afghanistan," said Gerry, "but good, yes, we'll run with Afghanistan."

"And next I thought we'd cover the bomb blasts in Israel," said the man.

"But the next pictures are of my wife's charity efforts?" said Gerry.

"Well I don't know what's going on with them," said the man, "but I really didn't think we should bother getting involved in a charity as such."

Gerry thought for a moment; "No, we should get this charity moving, it's a good cause and it's being run by my wife! So, get all the stuff you can on it and give it plenty of air time from now on." Gerry smiled to himself "Thanks dad," he said quietly.

Jimmy felt like he had accomplished something during his time-off, so he was ready to go back up to Andrew by this time.

Andrew chirped up at that moment. "Jimmy, while you're down there in that area, I have a special job for you. Can you fit it in?"

"Of course I can, Andrew," replied Jimmy, "what is it?"

"Do you remember your pal Freddy on the pipe-laying gang? The one who would never stop smoking, even when working near gas?" asked Andrew.

"Yeah, dear old Freddy Fag," replied Jimmy, "we used to call him a 'smoke-a-holic' because he always had a cigarette in his mouth. Why? What's up with him, Andrew?"

"You might guess!" said Andrew. "He's only working on a pipe joint at this moment, with no one with him, and he's lighting up a cigarette!"

"He's a nutcase if ever there was one," said Jimmy, "I'll get straight over to him now."

Jimmy arrived on the scene, to see Freddy light up his cigarette, as he sat astride the pipe.

"Freddy," said Jimmy, in a raised voice, just like he used to do when he was the foreman.

Freddy jumped and put the cigarette out quickly.

"Sorry, Jimmy," gasped Freddy, "force of habit you know."

"That force of habit will be the death of you one day, Freddy," said Jimmy sternly, "then who will look after your mother?"

"See what you mean, Jimmy," stuttered Freddy, "it won't happen again, Jimmy, I'll be careful."

"See that you are, my lad, or next time it will be you that's going up, instead of the price of gas!" said Jimmy.

Freddy watched as Jimmy walked steadily down the line of the pipe. He was doing his old job again, inspecting the line and making sure it was straight and to the plans!

Freddy was joined by his mate, who had come to help him to seal up the joint and test, before they backfilled the trench. They had to hurry now as the householder was waiting for the supply to be reconnected, and cook a meal.

"Jimmy has just been and looked over the job," said Freddy.

"You dimwit," said his mate, "can't have been Jimmy, he's been dead for years!"

Freddy remembered going to a funeral, and yes, it was Jimmy's funeral!

"How come, then," he said to his mate, "if, as we know, Jimmy is dead, how come he's just been here and told me off for smoking on the pipes?"

"Jimmy always had to tell you off for that, dickhead," said his mate, "'cause you're that daft in the head you'll end up blowing us all to kingdom come! You must have just been dreaming again, and Jimmy doing that was just part of your daydream!"

"Yeah, I must have," agreed Freddy, and then lit up his cigarette, as his mate turned on the valve to test for gas pressure and leaks.

There was a leak, as Freddy found out, and took the full brunt of it. His mate was thrown clear, about twenty metres away, but Freddy was stood looking at the hole in the pipe as Jimmy walked up to his side.

"You couldn't do as you were told could you?" said Jimmy.

"I'm, I'm sorry Jimmy, just habit I guess," said Freddy. "You know, I always seemed to be lighting up wherever I was."

"Aye lad, well this time you've had your last cigarette for good," said Jimmy, "and now you'll have to come with me, to the world after this one."

"Right, Jimmy" said Freddy, "anything you say, Jimmy, you're the boss."

With that, Freddy and Jimmy were with Andrew.

"You couldn't save him then, Jimmy?" asked Andrew.

"No, not this dumb head," replied Jimmy.

"How was your trip down memory lane then?" asked Andrew.

"Strange," said Jimmy, "really strange. To be there, and watch your family, even see yourself before all this. It was really strange."

"Going back for another visit?" asked Andrew.

"Don't think so, or at least, not just yet," said Jimmy, "come on, give me some more work, I'm growing lethargic. Anyway, this nostalgia thing isn't what it used to be anymore."

Andrew gave him another client and off Jimmy went to work again. Now Jimmy was working the whole field, not just in Britain, but international!

"A funny thing happened today at work, mum," said Gerry on the phone,

"I was in a meeting discussing the programme, and we couldn't decide on what to show. On the table was a pile of pictures and reports, all put in some kind of order by my staff. When we came to review them, they all came out different and Afghanistan was on the top. Marie's charity came out next! What do you reckon to that?"

"Your dad was here today and we chatted about you and Marie," answered Hazel quite casually.

"Mum," said Gerry, "you always imagine that dad is still around and that he talks to you. You know he's been dead for some years, haven't you got used to that yet?"

"Of course I have," answered Hazel sternly, "but he does come back and visit occasionally."

"Mum, I worry about you," said Gerry, "and if Martin heard you talking like this he'd have you locked away."

CHAPTER THIRTEEN

Ghost – The Movie?

"Jimmy, do you remember seeing a film when you were alive, called Ghost?" asked Andrew.

"Yeah, we liked it so much that we bought the video and played it quite often," replied Jimmy. "Why?"

"Well," continued Andrew, "you'll be quite familiar with the plot then, won't you?"

"Yeah," said Jimmy, "go on."

"It seems that a spirit is actually doing what that bloke in the film did, on the underground train. He's causing havoc down there for travellers and no one can stop him," said Andrew.

"So you want me to find him on the railway network and bring him in?" asked Jimmy.

"That's about the top and bottom of it," replied Andrew, "but get him sorted quickly, we've had some people praying about it. They must be Christians that travel on the train every day, and they've clicked on to what they should be doing – praying!" said Andrew.

"I'll go straight down there. Where is it?" asked Jimmy.

Andrew gave him the destination and Jimmy beamed himself down to it.

The station was quite well used by people travelling into the city, and at rush hour it was bedlam to say the least. Yet at night it was totally deserted and eerie. Jimmy adopted body mode and waited on the platform, so as not to look out of the ordinary. He was wearing a dark suit, raincoat over his arm and a newspaper in his hand, just like many of the other men that were waiting. The train came and everyone scrambled to get on, leaving Jimmy on the platform as the train departed.

"Well that was good wasn't it?" he said to himself, as he waited for the next one to arrive.

He managed to board the next train and sat on it to the end of the line. Then he got back on when it was ready to go the other way again. No one showed up! He rode the train for hours until the tea time rush hour, and then it was not until nearly the last train before anything happened.

As he sat reading his newspaper, which by this time was well thumbed, he heard people complaining about their papers being blown out of their hands, and their bags being thrown about. Brief cases were hurled across the carriage and hats were knocked off.

Jimmy saw the spirit of a huge man approaching from one end of the carriage, and it was the spirit that was doing all the damage. He looked to be about forty-five years old, well built, not very handsome, and dressed in what was once a dark suit and overcoat.

"He looks very similar to the man in the film," thought Jimmy.

"He does, doesn't he?" remarked Andrew.

Jimmy put his foot out to trip him, and he fell headlong in the aisle. This made him jump up with a surprised look, and snarled with anger in his face.

"Sorry old chum," said Jimmy casually in his typically English voice, "didn't mean to send you arse over tit like that."

"What? How did you do that?" yelled the man. "You're not supposed to be able to see me, never mind touch me! Who the hell are you?"

"Sorry if I upset your little party tricks old boy, but it really is naughty of you to be doing stuff like this to innocent people, trying to get to and from work," replied Jimmy.

"Who are you?" he yelled again, as he tried to pick Jimmy up with the lapels of his jacket.

"You can't do that to me," said Jimmy, "I'm stronger than you. I'll tell you what, let's get off at the next station and have a chat about this, if that's all right with you?"

"You son of a bitch, you're riding on *my* train and you think you can give me orders!" he yelled.

"Perhaps if you stop yelling and sit down for a moment, we can have a serious talk," suggested Jimmy.

"I don't want to talk to you! So get off my train, you bastard, and leave me alone!" he yelled.

Jimmy stood up as the next station came into view, and took hold of the man's sleeve.

"This is our stop my friend," he said calmly, and they were immediately on the deserted platform of an out of town station.

It was quite an eerie place at the best of times, but tonight it was worse. The man couldn't believe that Jimmy had taken him from the train, and wanted to know the hows and the why of what Jimmy could do.

"So who the hell are you?" he yelled again, and it echoed across the empty platform and down the tunnels.

"I'll tell you who I am," said Jimmy calmly, "I'm James De'Ath, and I've come to collect you and take you across."

"I can't go anywhere with you until I know what happened to me!" shouted the man.

"No use shouting and raving at me, old chap, it won't do you any good whatsoever. Let's just calm down and talk this through like two perfectly ordinary people."

"Ordinary! Ordinary!" he shouted again. "You call this ordinary? I was pushed under the wheels of the train, and I don't know who did it or why, and you want to have a cosy little chat! You must have chicken shit for brains! I didn't want to die, I was just about to get my promotion, and perhaps a bonus!"

"First of all," began Jimmy, "I can say no, this is not ordinary for me either, so I will show you all the answers to your questions, and then I'm going to take you across with me."

The man decided that he'd had enough, and kicked an empty drinks can at Jimmy. Of course, it passed right through him.

"You have to pump up a lot of psychic energy just to do that, don't you?" said Jimmy, as he made the can return to its original place without even touching it.

This didn't make his friend very happy, and he rushed at Jimmy with the intention of knocking him into the wall. He passed straight through

Jimmy and stopped. Jimmy took hold of him and lifted him from the ground, and as he let go, the man floated higher up towards the roof. Then Jimmy turned him upside down and brought him back to the platform.

This infuriated the man even more. "How can you do all that?" he yelled, as he tried again to hit Jimmy, in the face this time. Jimmy didn't even move or twitch.

"Garry," said Jimmy, "let's get down to business, because at this rate we'll be here all night, and I'm ready for something to eat."

"You can eat," asked Garry, "and how come you know my name?"

"Of course I know who you are, I've been sent down here to get you," replied Jimmy, "*and* I don't have to summon up all that psychic energy to do things like you do, because I *should* be here and you *shouldn't*."

"I don't believe you," shouted Garry, unsure really what to believe about this situation, "this is my station and my train!"

"All a thing of the past old boy, now," said Jimmy, "you're going to leave this behind just like you should have done two years ago."

He made another lunge for Jimmy, coming to rest just in front of his face. Jimmy used his thumb and finger to give him a flick on the nose, which didn't do any good, it made him angrier.

"Look, Garry," said Jimmy, "this has gone far enough. I'm not here to hurt you in any way, I've just got to ..."

He cut himself short as he dodged a flying waste bin, more out of reaction than fright. It clattered along the platform and emptied itself all over the place. Jimmy heard the sound of a train coming, and as it rattled through, Garry leapt on to it and sneered at Jimmy through the window.

He mimed these words through the window, "Bastard! Bastard! Bastard! Now let's see if you can get me!"

Garry went to the front of the train to start his usual business of disruption, but the driver turned round and said to him, "Don't do any more of that on *my* train, Garry Beldhart."

Garry turned in amazement to see Jimmy sat at the controls.

"How did you get here?" he yelled.

Then he and Jimmy were on the platform again, at the deserted station.

"Hey, bastard, how did you do that? Tell me!" yelled Garry.

"I've been trying to tell you all along," said Jimmy, "I'm not just a drifting spirit like you, huffing and puffing up the psychic energy to get about, I've been given more powers than you will ever have. I need them to do my job."

Garry still didn't get the picture, or rather, didn't want to get the picture, and summoned up enough energy to break the glass of the cigarette machine. Its contents fell out all over the floor.

"This is getting too much like the film," said Jimmy, "I wonder if the people who wrote the script actually rode on this train. Next you'll be craving for a fag, won't you?"

His words hadn't settled on the air before the man was crouching on the floor beside the pile of cigarettes.

"If only I could just have one of these again," he moaned.

Jimmy said to Garry, "Look mate, I'll show you something that you can't do."

Jimmy looked down the platform at all the litter, which had been blown about more by the last train. As Garry watched, all the bits of paper blew together and began wrapping themselves together, eventually forming the figure of a woman. Jimmy clothed her in something that Garry would recognise. Garry stared wide-eyed as it walked along the platform towards them both.

"Hi Garry," said the figure, "you're home from work early today?"

Garry mumbled something, and then said it out loud.

"Betty? Betty, what the hell are you doing here, you should be at home feeding the kids!"

She climbed into the open litterbin, and the figure fell back into pieces again.

"Hey, that wasn't very nice, you bastard," shouted Garry, "what do you think you're playing at with my wife?"

"Listen Garry," said Jimmy, but it was too late, Garry had managed to get the fire extinguisher from the wall to float across towards Jimmy.

"Take that, you bastard!" yelled Garry, thinking it would hit Jimmy on the head.

Jimmy caught hold of it and made it face towards Garry, and then he made it float towards him and stop near to his face. As it did, Garry looked sternly at it, and Jimmy made it discharge some of the contents into Garry's face. He spluttered a few more choice insults at Jimmy whilst wiping his face. By now he was covered in white down to his waist, and his thick black hair was matted together like straw.

Jimmy couldn't do anything else but laugh, which angered Garry at first, and then he seemed to see the funny side.

"Come on mate," said Jimmy, "let's at least be friends for a little while, after all, you've got no friends down here have you?"

Garry set off with his tale of woe.

"I had lots of friends! I had a lovely wife and two fine children! I had a regular job in a busy office and was looking forward to some promotion, and then I get pushed under a train for no reason. I never hurt anybody in my life! I know I'm not the world's most handsome man, but I was a kind and loving husband. I loved my kids with all my heart, and I reckon they'll be wondering where their father is right now! And now I've got you pestering about with my train, and ..."

"Yes," interrupted Jimmy, "ruining your somewhat bizarre attempts at revenge on someone, and you don't even know who!"

"What do you mean, I don't know who? It was those other people who were stood on the platform, the commuters who rode along with me every day! Course I know who!"

"You're wrong," said Jimmy, with a shrug of his shoulders, "you've been labouring under that misconception for all this time."

"OK big shot!" yelled Garry, "if you know all the frigging answers, perhaps you might enlighten me too, please!"

"I can do better than that," announced Jimmy, "as you should have realised by now. Why don't we become friends, and I'll *show* you the answers to all your questions, not just tell you them."

"Can you do that?" asked Garry, becoming a little calmer by now.

Jimmy told him to come with him, and took him back in time to the day of his death. The platform was filling up with commuters, and it was becoming quite crowded.

"Just look at you," said Jimmy, "you're a mess, Garry."

"You frigging did all this with that fire extinguisher, can't you do something about it?"

"I can't really take you anywhere looking like that, can I?" said Jimmy, as he changed him into the clean and sharp image of a city gent.

"Tidy hair, clean shaven, smartly dressed, now you look good enough to attend lunch at the Savoy," said Jimmy.

Garry was amazed and began to take Jimmy more seriously now.

As they watched from the end of the platform, they saw Garry come down the steps and onto the platform. He looked quite a lot like he did at the moment, but not as sharp!

"Hey there I am!" said Garry. "Will I be able to see myself or speak to my own body, because I could warn myself?"

"Of course not," said Jimmy, "think of yourself as an observer, without voting rights!"

Garry looked at Jimmy, and Jimmy grinned back at him. As they watched, they saw Garry's wife follow him down the steps at a safe distance.

"Hey, what's she doing at the station?" said Garry. "She doesn't go anywhere to work, she's supposed to be at home looking after the kids!"

They looked on as his wife shuffled through the crowd to get within arm's length of Garry, who was always on time and always at the front of the platform. The train rumbled through the tunnel to stop at the station, but before it had reached the place where Garry was standing, his wife nudged two people in the back, and made them push into Garry's back. This resulted in Garry falling off the end of the platform in front of the train, to the horror of all that were standing there.

She then pushed back through the crowd as everyone tried to see what was happening up front. She disappeared up the steps and vanished, and no one would ever know that she had been there.

"It was *her*!" exclaimed Garry. "But why? I never did anything wrong to her all of the time that I've known her. I work hard to get the money to pay for everything we have, and she's never gone without, all our married life!"

"Come on," said Jimmy, "let's go to your house."

They were there immediately, and Garry stared in amazement as he saw the empty rooms. All the furniture had gone, and each room was totally empty! Then they saw a real estate agent showing some people around the house. It was up for sale!

"Where's my wife and my kids, and my furniture?" asked Garry, quite confused by all this.

"Let me show you," said Jimmy, "then things will become clearer for you."

Jimmy took him to the house next door, the neighbour's house. There was some of his furniture, and his wife!

She was busy making a teatime snack, and then the children came home from school, very happy, and greeted their mother. Whilst they were eating their snack, in came Larry, the neighbour, and the kids were glad to see him.

"After you have had your meal, we're going bowling!" announced Larry.

The kids became excited and after leaving the table, grabbed a bag and put their very own bowling shoes into it.

"This all looks so natural," said Garry, "like as if I'm not being missed at all."

"You're not," said Jimmy, "in fact, you might say that when you were alive, you got in the way of your wife's happiness! She never really loved you, in fact, you just kept her in dollars until she could get rid of you."

"You don't say!" said Garry in amazement, "everything looks so natural, you'd think they were his kids and his wife! I've only been dead for a few years, too!"

"And you never suspected a thing!" said Jimmy. "She'd had this planned for years."

"No, never," agreed Garry. "So when does he get his 'reckoning' for his evil deed?"

"When he gets to the other side, mate, when he crosses over to where we're going," said Jimmy.

"Will I see him there? Will I remember what he's done?" asked Garry.

"Yes, you'll know him, and what he did, but it won't matter to you anymore, because you'll be different by then," said Jimmy.

"Get me out of here, Jimmy," said Garry, quite confused and disgusted.

In a split second they were back on the deserted station, with the wind from the tunnels blowing harshly across the front of the platform. Garry looked at the pile of cigarettes on the floor, in front of the machine that he had broken.

"I could just do with one of those right now!" he said to Jimmy.

Jimmy picked up a packet and opened it, took out a cigarette and popped into Garry's lips. It lit as he did so, and Garry inhaled a large volume of smoke. He blew out the smoke and inhaled again.

"Ooh that's better," said Garry, "but how come I couldn't do this before?"

"I told you," said Jimmy, "I have more special powers than you, it's all part of the job."

"So what now?" asked Garry, "my wife is living with my neighbour like I never existed, and my kids have forgotten me, so what's next for me?"

"When you've finished that, mate, I'll take you across and get you processed, then everything will be all right for you," said Jimmy.

Garry puffed on the cigarette, and then they left. The cigarette machine was restored to its former condition, and all the cigarettes were back in place.

The underground train's ghost had gone!

"You always have a personal way of doing things, don't you, Jimmy," said Andrew, "not like my other angels of death who just 'do their job' as it has always been done. Mind you, your clients always come over willingly!"

CHAPTER FOURTEEN

Voices From Beyond the Grave!

"What's that you're working on there, Andrew?" asked Jimmy. "Is it part of a new computer?"

"Sort of," replied Andrew, "but it's still in the trial stages yet. When it's ready, the people on the earth plane will have a direct link with people who have crossed over."

"What, like some sort of telephone to the dead?" suggested Jimmy with a wry grin.

"Well, yes, I suppose you could call it that, but it will be a little more complicated than just dialling up a soul," said Andrew. "It's called E.V.P., which stands for Electronic Voice Phenomenon."

"Electronic What-sits?" asked Jimmy.

"Electronic Voice Phenomenon is a way of speaking to people who have crossed over, but only for short messages. I've sent the idea down to the earth plane and an inventor is already making some headway with it. Mind you, he's had to put up with a lot of scoffing at *his* idea of speaking to the dead, but give it another thirty years and they may make something of it."

"What if they don't?" asked Jimmy. "And will it make any difference to us and how we work?"

"Oh I dare say it will be some time yet, but it won't do anything to the way we work. One inventor has taken up my method of using thirteen radio waves, which I've nicknamed 'Spiricom' to receive the sounds of the dead speaking. Another has a type of tape recorder that will receive the waves of sound. Don't forget, Jimmy, we can only put forward our technology in little doses, and let them work it out, otherwise, it would blow their minds. And, we have to give them the right of individual choice as to how they will eventually use it, that's His orders!"

"But what if they don't use something for the right reasons, say, the atom bomb, what happens then?" asked Jimmy.

"Well," said Andrew with a disappointed face, "we've already seen what happened with that technological invention, that was supposed to cure and save lives, haven't we? But after its initial use to stop the world war, it has become an unsafe and unfriendly deterrent that can easily fall into the hands of evil men."

"Yes," agreed Jimmy, "all too often we see countries threatened by the use of nuclear weapons by mindless dictators."

"Anyway, Jimbo," said Andrew, changing the subject with his usual humour, "how about you trying out this new telephone for the dead, then?"

"What, me?" replied Jimmy, "how can I contact anybody with a thing like that, I might just as well go down there and 'body mode' myself."

"It needs someone to help out in getting this thing off the ground, pardon the pun," said Andrew, "someone to try and get some people interested and see the use of it. It will be a great comfort to those who have just lost somebody, and want to know that they have crossed over safely."

"What about my day job?" protested Jimmy. "What if I get behind with that, what then?"

"Jimmy, you are more than just Mr Death to me, you are more like my left hand," said Andrew, secretly trying to boost up Jimmy's ego to do the job.

"Don't you mean *right* hand?" said Jimmy.

"Whether it is right or left, you are like my own personal champion, the best in the job. That's why I could trust this to you with all my confidence," said Andrew, with his arm around Jimmy's shoulder. "And just think, If you get this up and running to some extent that the earth people can continue to experiment, it will mean another commendation from you-know-who!" said Andrew with a cheeky grin.

"You crafty old codger! You're working me up to say yes, aren't you?" said Jimmy, catching on to what Andrew was angling at. "All right, I'll give it shot, but mind you, I know nothing about electronics!"

"Of course you do, my friend," said Andrew with an encouraging voice, "don't forget, you have your new mind since you were processed, and now you can understand everything."

"Of course I do, my friend," replied Jimmy with a less enthusiastic voice, "and yes I had forgotten about knowing everything because I've been doing just about everything that you put before me, haven't I?"

"Maybe so, but you are the best!" replied Andrew, quickly.

"Look," said Jimmy, "I know this is one of your little 'pet projects' again, like so many other things that mankind has had the misfortune to stumble on in the past. So all right, I'll have a go and see what I can make of it, if that will make you happy! Mate!"

"I knew I could count on you, Jimmy," said Andrew, all fussing and fumbling as he gave Jimmy a quick look at his manual for the machine. "Just take this manual into your mind and go and see if you can forward the invention along a little."

"Got it," said Jimmy, "and here goes Mr Electro De'Ath into action!"

With that, Jimmy was back on earth and walking along a street in Manchester. He bumped into a man coming out of a little electrical shop, who immediately apologised, as he was trying to come out backwards and close the door behind him.

Jimmy looked into his mind. This was one of the inventors that he had to meet up with.

"I'm very sorry, I was trying to do two jobs in one go, as usual," mumbled the little man as he struggled with some equipment that he had just bought.

"That's all right, mate," said Jimmy, "I wasn't looking where I was going either, I was window shopping for a couple of cheap PCBs with some zener diodes on them, and perhaps an electrolytic pack."

"Are you an electronics builder?" asked the man.

"Well, not really," said Jimmy, "but I'm working on a little project in my spare time."

"I do electronics, and I've found that this shop has plenty of bits and pieces, at the right price," said the man. "I'm Norris, pleased to meet a fellow inventor."

"I'm Jimmy, and it is nice to meet someone who shares the same interests. What exactly are you working on at the moment, because it looks like you've spent a fortune in there?"

"You'll probably only laugh if I tell you," said Norris.

"Well," said Jimmy, "it can't be any dafter than the thing that I've got on my mind, and started building."

"What's that then?" asked Norris, "if it's not too secret that is."

"Nah, you'll laugh at me if I tell you that I'm trying to build a machine to contact people that have died," said Jimmy.

"That's exactly what I'm doing!" exclaimed Norris. "How come you are as well? I thought I was the only one to have thought of this."

"Well apparently not," said Jimmy, "there's another bloke besides us two that's on with the same thing."

"Would you like to come home with me and have a look at what I've done so far?" asked Norris of his new friend.

"Sure would," replied Jimmy, "if you don't mind me doing that. Is it in the final stages or still just an idea?"

"Oh no," replied Norris, "I've actually had it working!"

The two walked off discussing electronics and caught a bus to where Norris lived, a small semi-detached house on the outskirts of the city. The little man fumbled with bags and keys and eventually gave up as the keys fell to the ground. Jimmy picked them up and unlocked the door, without knowing which key fitted the lock!

"That was good how you unlocked the door with the right key," said Norris.

"Pure luck I think," replied Jimmy casually, so as not to draw any further attention to his capabilities. Once inside, the house looked very neat and tidy with nothing out of place.

"Are you married, then?" asked Jimmy, "cause no man that I know could keep a house as tidy as this if he were on his own."

"Oh yes," replied Norris, "she's probably gone to the supermarket, that's her see, Janet." He pointed to a picture on a set of drawers in the lounge, as if Jimmy could see it from that far away. He led Jimmy up the stairs to a back bedroom, which was littered with every piece of gadgetry, parts, bits, pieces, odds and ends to do with electronics. There was an old television, which had been stripped for spares, and the body had been left where it had landed. Jimmy was impressed as far as seeing someone who was committed to a hobby to this extent.

"My word," exclaimed Jimmy, "you certainly take this seriously, don't you?"

"Oh yes," replied Norris, "but the wife won't come in here, not even to give it a quick dust round! Mind you, there's not a lot of surface area left, is there?" and he gave a little chuckle.

"My wife doesn't go into our garage anymore, where all my stuff is, either," returned Jimmy, "in fact, she doesn't even want to know about my hobby."

"Well, it might be for the best," said Norris, "they can sometimes get in the way of progress by moving things to different places, can't they?"

"You're not wrong there, mate," agreed Jimmy, "you can't find a thing when the wife's been in and tidied up."

Norris uncovered his machine at the far end of the bedroom, and Jimmy took a close look.

It was just like the picture that Andrew had planted in his mind, except for a few unfinished pieces, bits missing and some that were wrongly placed. That was where Jimmy would come in.

"Wow!" exclaimed Jimmy, "you have got on a long way with it, haven't you?"

Norris smiled, "Is it as far on as yours?" he said.

"Well, I think we're at about the same level, but you've got some things in here that don't look like they belong," said Jimmy.

"What do you mean?" asked Norris, with great concern in his voice, "I've been working on this for two years now, and I've had it working!"

"Bet it was all crackling and hissing?" said Jimmy without looking away from the circuit that he was studying.

"No!" snapped Norris. "Well, yes it does a bit, I suppose, but this is a completely new field in this kind of engineering, anyway."

"Maybe so, but look at this circuit here," said Jimmy, as they both got down to the bench and Jimmy removed the lid from the machine.

"According to your rough circuit drawing, this diode should be a 2.5 and you've actually got a 1.25."

"Let me see," said Norris, "you're right, but I wonder how that happened?"

"And that's not all, mate," continued Jimmy, "the hissing could be caused by this transistor, I've used two that are twice as big as this one."

Before many more minutes had gone by Norris produced a soldering iron, plugged it in and left it to warm up. Jimmy removed the pieces that were wrong and soldered some new bits into their places. Norris watched with wide eyes as his new friend redesigned his invention.

"Can we try it now?" asked Norris, keen to see what the difference would be with the new parts.

"Oh no, not yet," replied Jimmy, "look here, this thyrister has burnt out and wants replacing before we can crank it up."

"You certainly know your stuff," said Norris, "but does this mean we'll have to share the patent?"

"No, I'm not interested in marketing the thing, I just play about with stuff like this," said Jimmy. "You do whatever you want with it with my blessing."

Norris eventually plugged it in and switched on and there was a big bang before the lights on the machine faded out.

"What's happened?" shouted Norris, as a little puff of white smoke issued from the back of the box.

Jimmy lifted the lid off again, looked inside and smiled.

"It's only another resister that's blown, and that's only because it should have been an 8.00Mtz and you've put a smaller one in," said Jimmy with an encouraging smile.

It was replaced immediately after Norris had rummaged through a large box of bits in the corner of the room.

Once more, the machine was switched on and it seemed to hum into life, with all its little lights twinkling and flashing. Norris turned the controls and the two men waited for any sounds to come through.

"Shouldn't you be using the microphone first?" asked Jimmy quietly.

"Oh, of course I should," agreed Norris, "silly me, I haven't asked for anyone to contact us, have I?"

Sounds began to filter through, blurred at first, but they began to get clearer.

"The hissing and crackling has stopped," said Norris, quietly.

"Told you," agreed Jimmy.

Then a voice began to come through quite clear, though it sounded distant. Jimmy and Norris listened intently.

"It's working!" said Norris. "Listen, there's a voice coming through!"

Jimmy listened for a minute or two, then the voice became clear enough to understand what was being said:

"Jimmy, Jimmy, where are you?"

This was repeated three times and then began to fade away.

"She's calling to someone named Jimmy," said Norris, "isn't that great?"

"No," said Jimmy firmly, "because that's my name and it sounds like my wife's voice!"

"That's got to be a comfort to you, then, hasn't it?" asked Norris.

"Not when she hasn't died yet, or at least, not that I know of," said Jimmy with great concern. "I'll have to go mate, I think I'm probably needed elsewhere by the sounds of things."

Jimmy bade his friend farewell, walked across the room to the door and after closing it behind him, vanished back to Andrew's place.

"Jimmy, Jimmy," called Norris, as he tried to catch up with him on the stairs. Norris went down stairs and saw his wife in the kitchen.

"Did my friend just come through here, only he's had to leave and I wanted to get his phone number."

"No one's come through here all the time I've been in the kitchen, he must have gone out of the front door," said Norris's wife.

"He can't have, it's still got the security locks on it," said Norris.

Jimmy got back to Andrew.

"What's going on, Andrew?" he blurted, "I got the damn machine working and I heard Hazel's voice coming through on it, has she died?"

"No, no!" said Andrew. "She's not due for six years, three months and five days, twenty two hours and fifteen minutes. You must be mistaken."

"I know the sound of Hazel's voice, calling my name!" replied Jimmy.

"Just a moment," said Andrew, "it's here look. She hasn't died, but she has had an accident in the car, and although she is still alive, she is having one of those 'out-of-body' experiences. Go down to this place where she is laid on a hospital bed and get hold of her, before she ends up coming here before her time."

"Would that be a bad thing," asked Jimmy, "for me to see my Hazel again?"

"No, but it will bung up my computer for ages before I could get her back again," said Andrew.

Jimmy found the hospital room where Hazel's body was lying on a bed. Martin and Cath were already there, holding her hands and talking to the unconscious body. Jimmy smiled with a kind of thankfulness that said he knew they cared, and then slowly beamed himself up and out through the ceiling to find Hazel. Somewhere, midway between the two worlds, he saw her drifting towards him, big smile, calling his name. She wasn't bothered in the least about what had happened to her, she just wanted to be with Jimmy.

Jimmy took her by the hand and brought her to Andrew's place.

"Andrew, meet the wife, this is Hazel," said Jimmy casually.

"Hello, I'm glad to see you, Jimmy has told me so much about you, too," said Andrew.

"Jimmy, am I really DEAD?" said Hazel, still beaming with excitement. "Is this where you come to when you cross over?"

"No dear, you're not dead, and yes, this is where you will come when it is your time to cross over," said Jimmy. "The thing is, you haven't died, you are unconscious and having an 'out-of-body' experience, like you read about in those church magazines."

"But Jimmy, it feels so wonderful, I feel so free!" said Hazel.

"I've got to take you back, Martin and Cath are already at your bedside in tears, talking to your empty body," said Jimmy.

"Oh! I forgot about my family!" exclaimed Hazel. "How can I possibly put them through all this, while I'm here with you? It's so nice here though, Jimmy, I feel so good and peaceful, why can't it be like this on earth? I don't want to go back!"

"Hazel, dear, they won't know that all this has happened, and when you get back, they won't believe a word of it, will they?" said Jimmy.

"They never believed me about seeing you before, did they?" replied Hazel. "I will just have to wait until it's my time, then?"

"Afraid so, dear," said Jimmy, "then I'll come and fetch you, properly, and give you the guided tour myself."

"I will look forward to that, Jimmy Coney," said Hazel, "so don't go forgetting, will you? You won't forget to remind him, will you Mr Andrews?" she said to Andrew.

"No dear, he won't forget," said Jimmy, "now come on, say bye-bye to Andrew and let's get you back to your body. The children will be mourning you if we don't get a move on."

"It's so nice here, I don't want to leave," said Hazel, "I feel so peaceful."

Jimmy took Hazel by the hand and they were at the bedside, in the hospital ward.

"Look at them, Jimmy," said Hazel, still happy that she had seen him, "leaving them behind is the only thing that will hurt."

"Yes, I know what you mean, dear," agreed Jimmy, "that's the only thing that's bad about dying and crossing over, the people you have to leave behind. Anyway, how come you're in here?"

"A car pulled out in front of us as we were going to the supermarket, he hit the front corner and turned us over," said Hazel. "It was some young lads, joy riders I think, but I don't know what happened to them, or to Linda who was with me."

"The two lads in the other car have crossed over, dear," said Jimmy, "but look who's here?"

She turned to see Linda coming in through the door, with one arm in a plaster. Martin and Cath took hold of her and led her to a chair.

"She's still unconscious yet," said Cath, "the doctor said that all we can do is wait and hope and pray."

"She's a fighter," said Linda, "she'll pull through, just you see."

"Come on dear," said Jimmy, "they're all waiting for you, and it's not your time yet."

"I know," agreed Hazel "but don't forget to come for me, will you Jimmy?"

"I can't forget, I've got Andrew to remind me!" said Jimmy, with a sterner tone. "Now come on, in you go and get back to life again, for their sakes."

He let go of her hand and she returned to her body.

Martin rang the bell for the doctor as his mother began to regain consciousness, and the three visitors around the bed thanked God for answering their prayers. Jimmy watched for a moment as they hugged and kissed her, and then Hazel looked to one side as if she was looking for him. She gave a little wave, but it was only in case Jimmy was still there, as she couldn't see him any more.

It wasn't long before Hazel was back at home and fit again, although the car was too badly damaged to repair and was 'written off' by the insurance company. She attended the funerals of the two young lads who had caused the accident, and spoke to their parents afterwards. She told them that she would not blame them for the accident, and hoped that they could come to grips with their bereavement, reassuring them of a life after this one. They listened to her and thanked her for her concern, but they probably didn't understand all the stuff she told them about the after life. Neither did Martin and Cath, but Marie listened intently as Hazel related the story of her 'out-of-body' experience. It seemed that being of oriental descent gave her some kind of better understanding of spiritual matters.

"Hi Andrew, I'm back," said Jimmy.

"Oh, hello Jimmy my friend," replied Andrew, "you got her back in time then?"

"Yeah, no problem, apart from the fact that she keeps wanting to come back here," said Jimmy.

"Never before time, but always on time, that's how we like it," said Andrew.

"Anyway, what's happening with the inventor chap then, has he made a giant leap forward for mankind?" asked Jimmy with his usual comedy voice.

"Oh Jimmy, he's done really well since you got together with him, and they've formed groups and associations, and they've even started holding world-wide conferences," said Andrew, really excited.

"What, with a tripe invention like that?" replied Jimmy. "They must be out of their minds." Jimmy looked at Andrew, who was giving him a displeased frown.

"Err, well, sorry mate, I know it's your project for this decade so to speak, but couldn't you have thought of something a little more … well you know, sort of 'useful' as you might say? Anyway, what do you call a little square of mint chocolate that souls have after a meal?"

"I don't know," said Andrew, his interests and humour returning.

"An 'after life' mint!" announced Jimmy, and they both had a good laugh.

CHAPTER FIFTEEN

Jet Lag on a Higher Plane.

"Jimmy, I have a special one for you today," said Andrew, "one that will require a great deal of 'stage management' as you call it."

"Stage management?" answered Jimmy, a little offended, "Is that what you call my feats of masterly co-option of unsuspecting mortals to the spiritual habitats of the great beyond? And now, for your entertainment, the great Coney will perform another feat of magical mystery as he makes another mortal vanish into thin air!"

"No, no, no!" protested Andrew, "I didn't mean it like that in any way, shape or form. I simply meant that you have developed this 'art' of making the job a lot more interesting for those of us who are watching your progress."

"So it's quite entertaining for you then?" asked Jimmy, with a straight and displeased face.

"No, no," protested Andrew again, as he tried to get himself out of the corner that he had talked himself into, "not so much entertaining as more, well, we're delighted at the thought and care that you put into each and every job."

Jimmy smiled. "You crafty old codger, you're at it again! What's the job this time? Come on. Spit it out."

"Spit it out?" asked Andrew.

"You know what I mean," said Jimmy, "you've had the brain surgery up here, haven't you?"

"Well, it's like this," started Andrew.

"Here it comes," said Jimmy, "here comes the plot and the drawbacks! Tell me straight out."

"It's an airliner," said Andrew quickly.

"An airliner?" said Jimmy. "What, that's going to crash?"

"Well, not exactly, there's a bomb on board and no one knows. The whole plane will be blown to bits."

"That's awful, Andrew!" protested Jimmy. "Why?"

"It's the people on the earth plane who want to cause disruption and murder for political reasons," said Andrew, "we can't stop them from having free will to do what they want with their lives."

"Question!" snapped Jimmy.

"Yes?" replied Andrew.

"What have you done to Adolf Hitler then for all the political mayhem that he caused in the Second World War, answer me that!" said Jimmy, waiting for an answer such as 'we have retrained him and he's now an angel' sort of thing.

"If I told you, you wouldn't like it," replied Andrew.

"There, I knew it!" said Jimmy. "He's on some part of this complex where he's having a party of an after-life, isn't he?"

"No he isn't, but that's not our concern at this moment, it's the airliner crash," replied Andrew. "Now that I have your attention, let me fill you in with the details."

Jimmy listened to Andrew's idea of bringing two hundred and thirty people there at one go, after their aeroplane blew up in mid air.

"What if we do it my way?" said Jimmy, "it might be easier on the people involved, and more enjoyable for us."

"Jimmy, you're not supposed to enjoy your job like that," said Andrew.

"Well, I find that in making it easier for the mortals involved, getting them here without causing them any further stress, it does seem to be more enjoyable for me. And I like the challenge!" said Jimmy.

"Yes, all right my friend," replied Andrew, "we'll do it your way, whatever that is."

"Great," said Jimmy, back in the role of 'Ring Master' as he liked to be. "I'll need some help from an old buddy, so can you spare Dan for me?"

"Yes I think so, but what are you getting into this time?" asked Andrew.

"Leave it to me, matey, I'll get this show on the road and have your clients delivered to you in the twinkling of an eye!" said Jimmy.

Dan came to where Jimmy and Andrew were talking.

"Hi my good buddy, Jimbo, what's going down then, and why do you need my help?"

"Hi to you too, good buddy, it's great to see you again. I'm going to need a hand with an airliner. Ever done any flying, Danno?" replied Jimmy.

"Hey, I like the Danno, I might use that in the future," replied Dan, "then each time I bring a client up to Andrew, I can say ..." Jimmy joined in with Dan as he said, "Book 'em Danno!"

"No, that's not quite right Dan, is it?" said Jimmy. "It would have to be Andrew bringing clients to you, wouldn't it?"

"I guess you're right, Jimbo," said Dan, "but I haven't heard that said for an age, and I kinda like, miss it a bit, you know."

"You won't miss anything on this job," said Jimmy, "you're going to be in the cockpit with me."

"Wow, Jimbo, you mean that?" said Dan with excitement, "I can steer the plane, too?"

"Certainly can, co-pilot Danno," replied Jimmy, as the pair of them changed into pilot's uniforms, and their faces changed to those of the original pilots of the aeroplane.

Andrew smiled to watch the stage management of Jimmy's ideas take place, before they beamed down to the plane and were gone.

On the ground the plane was taxiing for take off. It was a wintry day, though the visibility was still very good and clear. Dan looked at Jimmy, and Jimmy at Dan.

"Well, don't just sit there Danno, get us off the ground!" said Jimmy as he switched a few switches, and wiggled a few knobs.

"Aye-aye, captain Jimbo," replied Dan, and they were off, up and away into the clouds.

"Hey, this is really something else, Jimbo's Jumbo," said Dan bubbling with excitement, "I've always wanted to be a pilot and fly these things around the world. If you get any more jobs like this, you won't forget to give your buddy a call, will you, Jimbo?"

"Of course I won't" said Jimmy, "I always liked working with you in the States, and I thought we made a good team then."

"Sure did, Jimbo, didn't we?" said Dan, "Hey, and didn't we have some fun, too, uh?"

"Sure did, matey," said Jimmy, "sure did."

"Anyhow buddy, what's going on with this plane then, and what's the plan for us and the mortals?" asked Dan.

"When we get over Scotland," said Jimmy looking at a chart on a clip board, "a bomb will go off in the luggage hold and blow the plane apart. To make it an easier transfer for the people on board, I thought that we could keep all their souls together on 'our' aeroplane and fly them straight into Airport Andrew. How about that?"

"Gee Jimbo," said Dan, with a big smile of approval, "that's such a great idea, and it could only come from someone who really cares about people."

"Stage Manager you mean," echoed Andrew's voice in their minds.

The two of them had a laugh as they flew over the Lake District and up towards the borders of Scotland, nearing the time for the bomb to activate.

The passengers had just heard a loud bang and were wondering what had happened. Some of them were standing up to look over the other passengers and out of the window. One shouted, "Hey, I can see some wreckage on the ground, it's a plane!" Everyone wanted to have a look, and scrambled to see through the small windows.

"That must have been the big bang," said someone. "It must have hit our plane!" said someone else. "If it had hit us, we'd be on the ground as well," said another man. People began to press the button for the stewardess, and wanted answers to their questions. The mood of the plane was changing from calm to panic. "We must be alright, we're still flying and nothing seems to be wrong!" shouted one passenger. "Will somebody tell us what is happening!" came the shout from a few passengers. There was a general agreement among them that nothing could be wrong, and then the stewardess reassured them that she would find out what had happened and give them all the full details.

The chief stewardess came to the cockpit and saw Jimmy and Dan flying the plane.

"You're not the pilots that got on at Manchester!" she said. "What's happened to them?"

"Don't panic my dear" said Jimmy with his 'kind' voice, "we are the proper pilots for *this* aircraft, and we are taking you to your destination."

"We're flying to America!" she snapped. "That's where we're supposed to be going!"

"Not any more, sweetheart," said Jimmy. "Sit down here and I'll explain everything to you, then you can help me to talk to the passengers."

She sat down and listened while Jimmy explained about the bomb, and told her that everyone on board was now deceased. At first she couldn't believe it, but then Jimmy showed her a couple of tests to prove that she was dead.

"Are you breathing?" he asked,

"Of course I'm breathing!" she snapped back, looking at Jimmy with a frightened anxiousness. "Wait a minute! No, I'm not breathing in and out!" She found a small mirror from her pocket and breathed on it. No vapour covered the glass. She started to get tearful, but then realised that she had a much tougher job to do with her colleagues and passengers, which seemed to take over her whole attitude.

"What shall I tell the others?" she asked.

"I'll tell them with you, then I'll make an announcement to the passengers," he said.

She called for the other stewardesses to come forward to the front cabin, and told the passengers to stand by for a message from the captain. Jimmy explained simply what had happened, and that there was no sort of 'option' or 'remedy' for the situation that they were in.

"How come you're so calm about it all?" asked one girl.

"I've been dead for some years, sweetheart, and I've got the job of helping people to cross over to the other side as easily as possible," replied Jimmy.

The way that she asked the question and the way in which Jimmy replied so simply made everything seem so natural. They didn't panic, but had a few questions to ask like, "what about our relatives, do they know what's happened?"

"By now, it's all over the news reports on the radio and television," replied Jimmy, "everyone is shocked and they have already started sifting through the wreckage and found all your bodies."

The girls were stunned by his frankness, but grateful in a way because he didn't give them a load of useless 'comfort' chat.

As they flew along in Jimmy's Jumbo, he made an announcement over the intercom and used the video screens to inform the passengers of the situation.

"May I have your attention, please, this is your captain speaking. As you will probably have heard a large explosion a few moments ago, I have to tell you that this aircraft is now flying a different course. If you looked down to the ground from your windows, you will have seen the wreck of the aeroplane that you boarded at Manchester."

The people were amazed to say the least. Some of them were saying things like, "It can't be, we're all right, and we are still flying. What's he talking about? Is this some sort of joke? It must be some other plane!"

Jimmy continued. "I'm sorry to have to tell you this, and I don't want you to panic in any way, as you ARE safe, but you have all died in the explosion and I am taking you to the after-life. You will be fine, and meet all your departed relatives, and we will get a message through to your loved ones to tell them that you are all right. Now, are there any questions? Yes, sir?"

"How come you say that we are all dead? We're just sat here, as we were when we took off. I didn't feel any pain, and I'm just enjoying what is to me a normal flight," said one man. A few others agreed, and then the whole plane erupted in chatter, with everyone finding it hard to believe what Jimmy had said.

"I can assure you, ladies and gentlemen, that is what has just happened, and I am glad that you all feel so comfortable. Our cabin crew will come round now to serve you with drinks from the trolley, free of charge! I hope that you enjoy the rest of your flight. Thank you very much."

Jimmy returned to the cockpit and Dan, with a face that said it all.

"What's up buddy?" asked Dan.

"They don't believe me!" replied Jimmy. "They think I'm having a joke with them! They don't realise that they are all dead."

"So what ya gonna do now then, Jimbo?" asked Dan as he continued flying the plane. "And where am I supposed to be flying this plane to?"

"They're all sat there drinking and chatting," continued Jimmy.

"Hey buddy" said Dan with some concern, "where am I flying this Jimbo's Jumbo to?"

"Oh, sorry mate," answered Jimmy, "I forgot all about you and the plane for a moment."

"I guessed that, Jimbo," replied Dan, a little anxious.

"Well, I'd better get some co-ordinates from the navigator, hadn't I? Mind you, if he doesn't know he's dead he won't know where he's going either, will he?" said Jimmy.

Jimmy looked at Dan, and Dan looked at Jimmy. Then the navigator spoke to them both and gave them the co-ordinates for Airport Andrew!

The two men looked in astonishment at the navigator, a balding, silver-haired man, who looked to be about six hundred years old! Andrew looked at them both from the navigator's chair, "Well, you don't mind if I share in one of your adventures, do you?"

"Hey, Andy, buddy, am I glad to see you, I was beginning to get a little ..."

"Scared?" cut in Andrew. "Scared, with your buddy Jimbo in charge? Never in this wide world, pardon the pun."

"Well, let's just say, a little anxious," said Dan in his own defence.

"I hadn't planned for the touch down," admitted Jimmy, "but it all seems to be going a little 'pear-shaped' now, because the people on board don't believe that they are dead."

"Just announce the imminent landing and seat belt procedure, Jimmy," said Andrew, "and they'll disembark as normal, regardless of the length of the flight time."

"Right away," replied Jimmy, and he made the announcement.

As they 'landed' at Airport Andrew there was a large crowd waiting in what looked like an airport building, all waving and looking out for relatives on the plane. The passengers left the plane with some amazement and were processed immediately, so that they understood what had happened. Then they met up with some of their relatives who were waiting for them. Andrew arranged for them to view some of the television coverage of the crash, so that they could see just how things were progressing on the ground. This would give them some kind of ease in their minds.

"Hey Jimbo," said Dan, "guess what?"

"Go on, I know your *dying* for a joke, pardon the pun," replied Jimmy.

"They've all come to the 'terminal' building," said Dan, "pardon the pun."

"It's a pity Andrew isn't here to listen to this," said Jimmy.

Just then, Andrew came towards them, laughing. "You pair make all this seem so pleasant, and joking about things like death. I've never had anybody doing this job like you two before, in my life, oh, pardon the pun."

Dan and Jimmy cracked out laughing again at Andrew's unknowingly witty remark, as he still hadn't grasped the fact that the two men had caught the habit of 'pardon the pun' from him.

CHAPTER SIXTEEN

Man's Best Friend.

Jimmy returned to Andrew's place after the aeroplane had vanished, and all the passengers were safely processed and dispersed.

"You know what," said Jimmy, "I felt quite uneasy when those passengers didn't believe that they had all died."

"It sometimes happens, Jimmy," replied Andrew "and really, there's not a lot you can do about it until they actually arrive here. I saw them being greeted by their relatives, just like they would have been if they had flown to America and landed in New York."

"I know," agreed Jimmy, "they didn't have a care in the world once they were off the plane! Mind you, that's what it's all about isn't it? You know, getting them across without causing them distress."

"Yes, that's right," agreed Andrew, "why cause them any more upset when they've just died?"

Jimmy was shaking his head in agreement when he noticed a wry grin on Andrew's face.

"You're having a go at me, aren't you?" said Jimmy, "you are, aren't you? And I bet it's about that guy on the underground train who kept trying to hit me."

"Well, it was quite funny to watch, you must admit," said Andrew with a laugh, "he tried all sorts of things to wreck your efforts, didn't he? But you still managed to gain his friendship and bring him in."

"That's what I went down there for, and there was no way that I was coming back on my own!" said Jimmy with a confident attitude in his voice. "Anyway, you were going to tell me about Mr Hitler before I went on the last job, so come on, out with it, where is he?"

"There is no time to tell you all the story now, but when you come back from this next assignment I'll give you an abridged version," said

Andrew.

"What about telling me now?" asked Jimmy.

"This is something more urgent," said Andrew, "a man in a park, he's about to drown and I need you down there quickly. Try and persuade him not to do what he is doing, it's not his time yet and he'll upset my programme for rehabs if he comes over now."

"I'm on it," said Jimmy, "but when I come back I want some answers about Mr H."

"Yes, yes, but go on your way quickly!" protested Andrew, as Jimmy vanished down to earth.

Jimmy dressed himself for the wintry weather, with a huge padded coat, boots, hat and gloves. He looked like a typical person braving the elements for a walk in the park. It had been snowing and the lake was frozen over, but not so hard that you could skate on it. It was more solid around the edges than it was a few paces towards the middle. Jimmy looked around and couldn't see anyone at first, and then he heard the sound of a dog barking across the other side.

He beamed in on the sound and was standing on the other side of the lake, where a dog had run onto the ice and fallen through. It couldn't climb back onto the ice to get away, and was clearly distressed by the cold water.

Jimmy looked around and wondered what he should do, when a young man came along the path and stood at the side of him.

"Is it your dog?" he asked.

"No, not mine, I've only just walked up to the lake myself," replied Jimmy.

The man began to call out to the dog, "Here boy, come on boy, you can do it."

The dog tried hard to scratch its way back onto the ice, but to no avail. The man carried on shouting as if he thought that he was encouraging the dog to try harder, "Come on boy, you *can* do it! Come on boy."

"We need to get some help, probably the fire brigade," suggested Jimmy.

"Yes, they would be the best," replied the man, "but I wonder how thick the ice is to where the dog is trapped."

"Don't try it, mate," said Jimmy, "if you go through there you'll be a gonner."

"We've got to try and help in some way, though," said the man, "I'll just tread carefully a little way out from the edge and I might be able to reach the dog."

"No!" said Jimmy. "Let me watch him while you go and get the fire brigade, don't try anything silly like that!"

"OK." agreed the man, and he went off to find a telephone.

Meanwhile, Jimmy walked across the ice and got hold of the dog and lifted it out of the water. He carried it to the bank and safety, then put it down. "There boy, now go on home and don't come back!" he shouted at it.

The dog shook the water from its coat and looked up into Jimmy's face, as if to say, "thank you mister." Jimmy looked around and was just about to beam himself back up to Andrew when the young man returned.

"I've phoned them and they'll be here in a few minutes," he said, and then he noticed that the dog was standing next to Jimmy. "Has he got out by himself?" he asked.

"Yeah," replied Jimmy, "the daft thing scrambled out as soon as you'd gone down the path. I told you it wasn't worth risking your life for it, didn't I?"

"Suppose you're right," agreed the man, "but it seemed like it was going to drown or die from the cold, and I love animals, don't you?"

"Well, I don't dislike them," said Jimmy, "but I never had a pet of my own, ever. They take a lot of looking after and then they die and you've got the upset with the missus and all that."

"I like dogs," said the man, "got two of my own, and two children."

"Well, nice to have met you, but I've got to be going now," said Jimmy, as he prepared to walk away and leave the man to wait for the fire brigade.

"Yes, nice meeting you, see you again, mate," said the man.

"I hope not, at least, not yet," said Jimmy under his breath.

Just then, as Jimmy turned to walk away, a small duck slid across the ice and dropped into the water to have a swim around. The dog made one long jump onto the ice and slid across to where the duck was. The duck flew off, and the dog dropped in. Jimmy looked on in amazement. "Daft animals, dogs, aren't they?" he said to the man.

"I think he's really in trouble this time though," said the man, "we ought to try and get him out."

"Leave him there till the fire brigade get here!" said Jimmy, sternly. "Don't go trying anything that might endanger your life for the sake of that daft thing!"

"Well, if I tread carefully, and you hold my coat sleeve, I think I could just about reach him," said the man, as he started to slowly edge across the ice.

"Come back, lad!" shouted Jimmy, "it's not safe for you!"

Another step took him to a short length away from the dog when there was a loud crack, and the ice gave way beneath him. A yell later and he was in the water, up to his neck, and the dog began to paw at him to try and get hold of him, so that he could stay above the water. The fire brigade arrived, as man and dog fought together in an attempt to keep their heads above water. They ran ladders across the ice to reach them, but as they got nearer, the man and the dog disappeared under the icy water, and under the ice.

Two of the firemen braved the cold water and dived in to look for them, but after only a few minutes, they had to get out and be warmed up again, as the water was freezing cold.

Jimmy stood on the bank, watching what was happening and pleading for them to find the man at least.

"It's all going wrong, Andrew," said Jimmy under his breath.

"Don't worry," Andrew replied. "If they don't save him I've found a little niche in the programme that I can fit him in. It's just that he's going to be too early, and I don't like that for the sake of the loved ones that they leave behind."

"Shall I perform some of my special stuff and get him out?" asked Jimmy.

"No, you can't do that," replied Andrew, "it will change things and deny the man his basic right of free will."

"What," said Jimmy, "it's his free will to die in this lake?"

"Yes, he decided to go onto the ice, it was his decision to take the risk," said Andrew, "and we have to respect his choice of free will, as you know, even when it leads to destruction."

"I could reach right in there and pull him out!" said Jimmy.

"No you can't," replied Andrew, "because using your powers will not be allowed to overcome the mortal's right of free will, you see, that's the 'law' of things."

Jimmy moved out of the way of the fire and rescue team, and changed into 'spirit' mode so that he couldn't be seen by anyone. Coming along the path around the edge of the lake he saw a man jogging, with a dog, trotting alongside him.

"Oh no," thought Jimmy, "they're too late, and they haven't found them in time!"

"Hi mate," said the man, with a big smile on his face, "I got the dog out, look."

"You bloody dimwit, you must be dafter than the dog!" said Jimmy. "Don't you know what's happened to you?"

"Yes," replied the man, "I climbed out of the other side of the lake and pulled the dog out too!"

"You're DEAD now, you soft article!" said Jimmy. "Look there, they're still trying to find you in the water!" Jimmy drew his friend's attention to the fire and rescue men, who by this time had just found the young man's body. A news team had also arrived and begun to transmit a broadcast to the television centre. Onlookers gathered in great number too! It had become a big event. They hauled the body of the man onto the side of the lake and tried to revive him, but to no avail. They covered the body with a blanket and pulled it up over his face, but not before a few cameras had flashed.

"Is that *me*?" asked the man.

"Yeah," replied Jimmy sternly, "that's what has happened to you for trying to rescue that bloody dog, instead of waiting for these chaps to arrive!"

"Am I really – dead?" he asked nervously.

"Well you're not laid under that blanket having forty winks, are you?" said Jimmy, "because you're standing here with me, now!"

"Well, who are you then if I'm dead and I'm standing here with you?" asked the man, nearly too frightened to ask.

"I am James De'Ath, I've come to take you across to the other side now that you're dead," replied Jimmy.

"But you were with me on the lakeside when I was trying to get to the dog, you weren't dead then were you?" he asked.

"Of course, I was dead then, I've been dead for years, and now you're bloody dead as well, through your stupidity!" replied Jimmy.

"I don't get this," said the man, "you were already dead but I could see you, now I'm dead and I can still see you? What about the firemen, can they see you, or me?"

"No! They can't see you or me, or the daft dog any more, because they've just pulled you out of the lake," replied Jimmy, who by this time was quite upset at the fact that a young man had given up his precious life for a dog!

"But if I could see you when I was alive," continued the man, "how come no one else can see you now that you're dead?"

"Look," said Jimmy, as he put his arm around his shoulders, "I was sent here to try and prevent you from dying in that lake. When I first met you I was dead, but allowed myself to be seen by people. Now that you're dead too, I can go back to being dead and not let anyone else see me except you. Does that make any sense to you or am I going round the twist here?"

"Oh, I get it," said the man, "when you were first dead I could see you ..."

"Look! Now you're dead. I can see you and you can see me, right?" said Jimmy. "Nobody else can see either of us, right?"

"Yeah," replied the man, vaguely.

"Bloody hell it's no wonder you went in after that daft bloody dog," said Jimmy in despair.

"I don't get this at all, I'm going home and you can get lost, you're mad," said the man.

"You think I'm mad," said Jimmy, "come on I'll take you home."

"Oh, have you got a car?" asked the man.

"We don't need a car," replied Jimmy, and immediately translated them to his home, looking in at the window.

Jimmy saw his young wife, getting a meal ready for two young children. It nearly made tears come to his eyes to see the family scene, knowing that it would never be the same again for them and all because of the foolishness of her young husband.

"There's Sally," said the man, as he tried to open the front door but couldn't turn the handle.

"Hey what's up here?" he said, somewhat alarmed, "I can't turn the door handle." He began knocking on the door, but there was no sound.

"Now do you believe me?" said Jimmy, this time a little more compassionate.

"Am I really dead?" he asked, "but what will happen to my family, I want to be with my family!"

"Sorry mate, your time's up on this plane," said Jimmy, and beamed them both up to Andrew.

Andrew looked at Jimmy, almost expecting to see tears, but Jimmy was more angry than sad for the young man.

"What a waste of life," said Jimmy, "couldn't we have done something to help?"

"Afraid not," replied Andrew, "that's how it goes. I can tell you this though, his pretty young wife will be comforted by a special friend of the family who helps her through it all, and eventually marries her."

"Andrew, that's all I wanted to hear, thanks a lot mate," said Jimmy, relieved. "Anyway, what's happened to that dog, where's that gone?"

"Animals don't always stay here, they're usually returned to the earth plane as 'young' again in the womb," said Andrew, "but sometimes they stay with their owners, and sometimes we put them onto the other level with all the other animals."

"You mean that there is another level with all the animals on it?" asked Jimmy.

"Oh yes," replied Andrew, "you can visit it at any time and see all sorts of animals, it's just like going to a massive zoo at times. If an animal is taken for food, they are usually put straight back into the chain, for food again."

"Well, I never imagined anything like that," said Jimmy, "I'll have to go and see it sometime."

"Yes, you will," said Andrew, "and what about all that swearing you were doing, where's that coming from, then?"

"I don't know," said Jimmy, "I never used to swear on earth, even when I got really angry, yet now and then it just pops out!"

"I could do something about it for you if it gets worse," said Andrew, "but sometimes, it sounds quite comical listening to you."

"You were having a laugh, again?" said Jimmy.

"No, no my friend, it's just that I can hear you all the time and it makes me chuckle to see you getting all worked up, when you've no need to."

"Does anyone else hear what's going on," asked Jimmy.

"Well, when I start chuckling, some of the other processors tune in to see what's making me laugh, and then they start chuckling too."

"Blood . . ."

"Careful now, Jimmy, you don't want to let someone else hear all those nasty words, do you?" said Andrew, grinning like a Cheshire cat.

"Oh well, I suppose I'm still good for fun, aren't I?"

"Of course you are," agreed Andrew, "you've always liked a laugh and a joke, Jimmy, haven't you?"

"Yeah, I suppose so," agreed Jimmy.

Just then, Jimmy felt something nudge the seat of his trousers, and turned around quickly to see what it was, just in case Andrew was playing some trick on him.

It was the dog from the lake!

"I think he's become quite attached to you," said Andrew, "do you want to take him on some jobs with you, he'll be good company."

"Not bloo—likely," snapped Jimmy, "what do you think I am, 'dog's best friend' or something? No way!"

Andrew grinned, and some of the other processors chuckled too, then he touched the dog's head and it vanished.

"Where's he gone now?" asked Jimmy. "He won't keep turning up all the time will he?"

"No, he's en route back to the earth plane again now, as a new born puppy," said Andrew, "but he would have made you a good partner, just like, what was that film? Oh yes, K9!"

"No way, Andrew," said Jimmy, "I don't really like dogs, and I don't need one for company! Anyway, I've always got Danno!"

CHAPTER SEVENTEEN

Paradise Cruise Liners

Hazel was in town and spotted a notice in the window of a travel shop. It read, 'Spoil yourself with a cruise around the Med'. "That sounds good," she thought, "I'll pop in and get some more details."

The travel agent sat her down and explained everything to her. He showed her the coloured brochure with pictures of the countries that the liner would stop at for a day or two. She had never needed to book a holiday herself, or for herself, as Jimmy had always been the one to spot the bargains and come home with the booking form. She hadn't felt like going on holiday anyway, as it wouldn't be the same without him.

The price was right and the holiday looked great, but she thought that she had better run it past the children first, to see what they thought. They might even want to come along too! She rang Martin and Gerry and asked them to come over for tea, and they both said that they were free that same evening.

"What's wrong, mum, why have you asked us all to come over to your house this evening?" asked Martin, a little apprehensive.

"There's nothing wrong," answered Hazel, "it's just that we haven't had a great deal of time to talk with each other lately, everybody being so busy, and I wanted to ask your advice on something."

"You're not short of money or anything are you?" asked Martin. "I reckon we got Dad's pension sorted out nicely for you, didn't we?"

"Oh it's not money," said Hazel with a smile.

"You haven't been talking to dad again, have you?" asked Gerry.

"Leave her alone, Gerry," snapped Marie, "I believe what she says when she tells me that she can hear him."

"It might not be a good thing to have these sightings and whatever," said Gerry. "It shouldn't be happening!"

"I know what I see and hear, Gerry," said Hazel, "and I'm not losing my marbles or going senile. If your father wants to talk to me, or pay me a visit he does, and I love him for it. He's still thinking of me, and I still think of him, every day."

"Maybe so, but it can't be healthy for ..."

"Gerry, leave it!" snapped Marie. "Just because you can't believe your own video film doesn't mean that your mother is wrong too!"

"OK!" said Gerry, defeated, "I'm sorry, I didn't mean to upset you, it's just that ..."

He caught a sharp look from Marie, which stopped him in his tracks.

Hazel continued, "I am thinking of taking a holiday, a cruise around the Mediterranean, in June, what do you think?"

"What, on your own?" asked Martin.

"Well, unless you and Gerry, Cath and Marie and the children want to come as well?"

"That sounds great," said Cath, "but I don't think I would like to take the children on a ship, not while they are so young."

"Yes, I see what you mean," agreed Martin, "but the idea of you going alone doesn't sound too good to me, either."

"She'll be alright," said Gerry, "she'll have dad with her, won't she?"

Marie gave him a dig in the ribs and another sharp look.

"I cannot have any time off around then," said Marie, "we're really short of staff at the moment, and we are waiting for the next batch of trainees to come through the training school."

"I'm sorry mum, too, it's not convenient for me, around then," said Gerry, "but it would have been great for us all to go away together."

"Yes," agreed Martin, "a family holiday like that would be nice, with Linda and Burt, too."

"Linda and Burt *are* going with me," said Hazel, "I just thought of asking you all as well. Anyway, after this cruise, we can organise one when we can all go, can't we?"

The family agreed that they would strive to get together for a family holiday, one day soon! Hazel had already arranged it with Burt and Linda, who were only too pleased to go with her. It was to be Burt's retirement celebration too! Although he was sixty years old, he still had that oriental, handsome look, and didn't look like a man who was sixty years old at all!

From booking the holiday in March, it soon came around to June, and the departure date. Burt and Linda were packing Hazel's luggage into the boot of their car, and everyone was definitely in an excited holiday mood. Marie was on her way to work and wished them all a happy holiday. She was driving them to Birmingham airport where she was working from, that week. She would have liked to have gone with them on the cruise, as it would have made a big change from flying everywhere. Martin and Cath phoned to wish them all well, Martin from work and Cath from home. At last they were all ready, and the car set off for the airport. Marie got them through the usual queues a little quicker than normal, as she knew the people on the checking in desk. Anyway, this was family! The plane took off for Athens, where they would join the ship.

"It's all rather like the film 'Titanic' isn't it?" said Linda, "we'll be on board a huge ship and nothing to do but enjoy ourselves."

"Aye," replied Burt, "unless we hit an iceberg."

"Oh don't be daft," said Linda, "there aren't any icebergs in the Med, just lovely hot and sunny days."

"I can't wait," said Hazel, "we always fancied a cruise when Jimmy was alive, and I promised myself that one day I would do it."

"You still miss him, don't you?" asked Burt.

"Yes, but I do know he's all right and he's thinking of me," replied Hazel.

Burt was oriental, and their families believe in the after life and all things like that, much more than the English people do. He was quite comfortable with the fact that Hazel had seen Jimmy, and talked with him. Linda just took his word that Hazel was not going insane in any way.

The plane landed at Athens airport, and the bags were swiftly collected and placed on a big coach, which took them to the docks. Hazel and Linda couldn't believe their eyes when they saw the size of the big, white cruise ship.

"Is this as big as the *Titanic*?" asked Linda.

"No," replied Burt, casually, "bigger!"

"Wow!" said Hazel. "It's going to take us a fortnight to get right around the ship!"

"It's going to take us a fortnight to get to our cabins!" said Burt.

The porters had everything under control and the luggage and passengers reached their cabins in no time at all. And what cabins! Burt, Linda and Hazel stood in the doorway and looked with amazement at the roomy, comfortable five-star cabin that had been allotted to the three of them. Hazel was sharing a family room with Burt and Linda, so that she didn't have to be on her own. It was so huge and spacious that there would have been enough room for the rest of the family.

"This must be a mistake," said Hazel, "this looks like a first class penthouse, not something that you get from our travel agent! Can we get it checked out before we set sail?"

"Too late, lass," said Burt, "we set sail fifteen minutes ago."

"But I didn't hear the engines start up, or feel any movement!" said Hazel.

"Me neither!" agreed Linda.

"What did you expect?" asked Burt, surprised. "We're not on a wooden cruiser on the Thames, ladies! This is the real thing, a ship!"

"I know," said Linda, "but you would have expected to hear someone shouting something, like, 'cast off' or something, wouldn't you?"

"They're running a ship, not knitting!" said Burt.

"Oh, very funny, very funny," said Linda, "you know what I mean, like in the films where they're all standing on the decks and waving."

"Yes," agreed Hazel, "that's what I expected to see."

"That's ok if you wanted to stay up on deck and wave to no one that knows you," said Burt, "but I'm off to the bar! I'm not doing any driving for two weeks, and I'm going to make the most of it."

"Oh you are, are you?" said Linda. "Well you can wait till we're ready so that we don't get lost. And we can have a look around the boat, too."

"Ship," said Burt.

"That's what I said," answered Linda.

"No," argued Burt, "you said boat and this is a ship. It's too big to be a boat."

"Jimmy would have said the same thing, Linda," said Hazel, "I sometimes wonder whether that pair used to rehearse their conversations together, they sound so much alike!"

"Yes, I see what you mean," agreed Linda, "now we're ready, Burt, lead the way."

Burt produced a map of the ship from his pocket, and studied the first part of the third deck of the second phase of the penthouse suites, that were on the upper circuit of the rear quarterdeck, behind the ballroom and the bar. Then he admitted to being lost!

The three of them were given a condensed tour of the ship by one of the stewards, who had been designated to their corridor of cabins. After that, Burt found a bar and they all stayed there for a while. The drinks were included in the price, in fact, everything they could eat or drink, or watch on a stage was included in the price. All they had to do was enjoy themselves!

It took the trio a day or so to find their way around, enough to get back to their cabin by nightfall. By this time, the ship was docking for the first visit at Sicily where they would have one full day to look around. Burt automatically became the tour guide for the two ladies, and tried to find all the best places to see, eat and drink. This he did with some ease, as though he knew where everything was. It was only because he had studied the itinerary of the cruise before they set off, and had got the information from the travel agent. But the women didn't know, they just thought that Burt knew all about these different places.

Back on board ship at the end of the day, the trio of travellers were very tired and ready for bed. The ship set sail again as they slept and was docking in Tunisia as they woke up the next morning.

"We have one day in Tunisia, ladies, then it's off to The Holy Land and Jerusalem," said Burt, the appointed tour guide.

"Where's Tunisia then, Burt," asked Linda, "is it near to Majorca?"

"No, it's on the north coast of Africa, between Algeria and Libya," answered Burt.

"What! We're in Africa?" said Linda, surprised, "will we be able to see some lions and tigers and suchlike?"

"You won't see anything like that here, you have to go on a safari to see them," replied Burt, a little disgusted at her ignorance, but it made Hazel laugh.

The day belonged to Burt again, who led the two women all over the place and fed and watered them at regular intervals. That night, they returned to the ship once again, tired and totally exhausted. They showered and changed, and then went up to the dining hall for evening dinner. Hazel and Linda loved the entrance to the dining hall, as it resembled that of the *Titanic* enough for them to make a comment every time they came to it. It was very plush and posh, yet everyone was extremely friendly and polite. Linda and Hazel tried to act the part of the rich people on holiday, but were sadly let down by Burt who wouldn't play along. He kept asking for a pint of beer instead of a glass of wine, and made one or two quite audible belches after long drinks of it. When the women put on a slight air or grace in their voices to impress the waiters, Burt would use some of his North London slang words to compensate. It was most annoying!

Linda would say, "May one have another glass of wine, please?" to the waiter, and Burt would add on, "Aye and mine's a pint, mate."

The evening was concluded by a visit to the theatre where a singer was on stage, and later there was a comic and a magician. It was all so 'out of this world' that the women found it hard to believe that such a life could be going on around them and they never knew or experienced it. It was definitely like another world.

Burt laughed a lot at the comedian, and all three of them were quite stunned by the magical illusions of the magician.

"I thought Paul Daniels would take some beating, but this bloke comes close," said Burt.

"Oh you and your Paul Daniels, that's the only magician that you've heard of anyway," said Linda.

The show went on till nearly midnight, and then the Captain came onto the stage and made a special announcement, as he had done at the dinner hall and the cinema.

"Ladees and gentlemen," he began in his best English, as he was Greek, "we will be zailing un eet tomorrow for the five days to get out at the Holy Land and veezit za Jerusalem by couch. Zees vill taken us then to Cyrpus before we go on back to the Greece. I weesh yous all a good tripe and enjoy your holidays. Thank you and good night."

Burt couldn't stop laughing at the way he spoke, and was repeatedly rebuked by Linda, until Hazel caught the laughter bug and started tittering into howls of laughter as well. Linda tried to calm them both down, but when she tried to reason with the pair, she burst into laughter as well. Burt began to imitate the Captain by saying things like, 'ladeez' and 'veezit za' until all three of them were holding their stomachs with laughter pains.

They had calmed down by the time that they got back to the cabin, and literally dropped on their beds and slept.

The next morning, the three of them woke up still wearing their evening attire. Linda looked at Burt and he at her.

"That was a good night, wasn't it?" said Linda.

"Sure was dear," replied Burt, as Hazel staggered out of her room into the lounge, fully dressed!

"I must have slept in my ... Oh, you're both dressed too!" said Hazel.

They laughed and vowed to do it again tonight. All agreed, and then went into their rooms to shower and dress for breakfast. After all, they couldn't go to breakfast in their evening wear, could they?

After breakfast, they had a stroll around the various decks, and did a little shopping, a little drinking, a little sun bathing, and a lot more drinking. The days were slow and leisurely, and all you could see from each side of the ship was, sea! They all thought that it was a long cruise down to the coast of the Holy Land, but what a great day out it would be when they get there. Burt had already secretly read up on the tourist spots, and the places of interest.

The days seemed long as they played games on the deck, swam in the pools, relaxed at the bars and generally enjoyed every minute of the holiday. Each night they would occupy the same seats in the theatre where they could best see each act perform.

It seemed like everybody else did the same too, and Burt always seemed to end up sitting next to a medium built Irish man with sandy coloured hair. He and his wife always sat in the same seats. After a couple of nights they got to know each other and spoke like old friends whenever they met. He also sat across from them at dinner, as the favourite places worked the same in the dinner hall, too.

The five long days passed and the Holy Land could be seen from the rail of the ship. Burt and the ladies dressed for the hot sun with hats and shorts, and plenty of sun cream on their faces. A long line of coaches waited to take people from the ship into Jerusalem, each one having a courier who doubled as a bodyguard. There was no trouble at the time, but every care had been taken to ensure the safety of the ship's passengers. Burt liked the idea, as it gave him a little breathing space in his job as tour guide if someone else had been appointed for that job already.

The tour was great! The trio wandered around the tourist places and saw all the marvellous things that they had only seen before on the television. Before they went to the 'Wailing Wall' it was customary to purchase a little hat to place on your head, like the Jews. Custom or politeness, it was a 'souvenir' more than anything! They stopped at a little market stall where everyone was buying these little head coverings, and each of them bought one. The man behind the stall had an assistant, and they were arguing with each other, in between serving customers.

"You'll have to excuse my partner, Manny," said the older man, "he's a German Jew and they always think they know more than the Jewish born Jew."

Burt had a laugh with them about it while the ladies looked on and listened. It was apparently their way of attracting the visitors, by pretending to argue and give some of the head coverings away at half price. It worked, because before many minutes had gone by, there was a crowd gathering in front of the stall. They sold all kinds of sun hats, head coverings and black hats for the Jewish men folk.

"You're on a winner at this," shouted Burt, "selling hats to the Jews."

"You betcha life we are," replied the older man, while his younger partner just kept on selling to the crowd.

"It must be like selling water in a heat wave," shouted Burt.

"I'll tell you something," said the Jewish man, "so long as the Jews have their religion and Jesus Christ doesn't come back I might end up as a millionaire!"

The crowd laughed as Burt taunted him further.

"What would happen if Jesus Christ did come back?" shouted Burt. By this time the man and his partner were doing a good trade, but he still wanted to keep the rapport going with Burt, and did for quite a while.

"If He came back?" he replied as if to question. "Shish! This load of religious nuts would have something to really start wailing about." The crowd roared with laughter. "I'd be out of a business and out of here like Jessie Owens." The crowd roared again with laughter. "And Manny Cohen here, well, he'd go back to Germany to teach history. He thinks he's descended from Adolf Hitler anyway!" The crowd loved it and cheered as Manny took a bow. It was all so well done and the ad-libbing was such smooth and natural comedy!

Hazel looked at Manny and couldn't help but think that he *did* resemble Adolf Hitler, but why would Adolf Hitler or any of his relatives be Jewish, and why would they be in the business of selling head coverings! When his turban was pushed back in the heat to allow him to wipe his forehead, his black hair fell across his forehead and was trapped there by the turban. She could almost see a small moustache under his nose and was quite taken back by her imagination. Or was it her imagination? "Oh, this is all so silly," thought Hazel, "I'm getting caught up in the joking of a market stall holder," and she walked away in disgust at herself for thinking such silly things. Adolf Hitler, a Jew! Nonsense!

Burt gave each of the women a little head covering and they went to see the wall, where the Jewish religious leaders went to pray every day. It was different from seeing it on the television, as the atmosphere was thrilling! Burt took some photographs, in fact, he'd taken loads of photographs wherever they went, even on the ship. He found a little café where they could have something to eat and drink, before getting back onto the coach to go back to the ship.

"All aboard the couch," said Burt as they reached the door of the coach, echoing the Captain's poor English. Some other passengers realised what he was saying and joined in laughing.

As always, they had walked quite a few miles whilst seeing all that they could fit in on their visit.

Once they were back on board ship it was a shower and relaxing time, before they went along for evening dinner. The trio dressed up as usual and sat at their usual table, next to the Irish man and his wife. It was just like being at home, or going down to the Club in the evening and sitting with old pals at the same table every time.

During the evening, the Captain gave his customary report on the itinerary of the cruise, and told them where they were going next. Everyone knew already, as it told them in the brochure, but the Captain always made his announcements.

"Ladeez and gentlemen," he began as usual, "tomorrow we will be coming upon ze Island of Crete, and then we will be coming back to Athens where your couches will taken you to ze airport. My crew and myself hoping you have had splendid holiday aboard The Paradise Cruise Liner. Thank you and good day."

The trio and the Irish couple were doubled up with laughter, and began to quote pieces of his announcement to prolong the laughter.

As Burt looked up from laughing the waiter was standing by the side of the table. "Can I get something for you else," he said in broken English.

Burt couldn't stop laughing, but eventually did for long enough to ask for another round of drinks.

Then the waiter said in a clearly Birmingham accent, "Yow ol' right there then, an' it's bitter for you, aint it mite?"

Burt's face was frozen for a few seconds, until Hazel, Linda, the Irish couple and the waiter all burst out laughing at him.

"You're a Brummie!" yelled Burt. "A flaming Brummie out here!"

"Well, yow can't talk like this and get the tips, can ya?" said the waiter.

"You can with us, mate!" shouted Burt, pleased to hear a familiar accent, "you can with us."

This just added to the enjoyment of the whole holiday, and none of them wanted it to end.

"We've just got to book another cruise like this," said Linda, "it's been really good fun and enjoyment all the way, hasn't it? I'm glad you talked us into coming along with you, Hazel."

"I've really enjoyed it too," said Hazel, "and I never dreamed that it could be such a good time, without Jimmy. It's the first holiday I've been on without him."

"Well, I've tried to do my best to see that you have a good time, and probably help you to get over him a little better," said Burt, "but no way would I ever suggest that you try and forget such a brilliant man and my good friend!"

"Oh, that's nice Burt," replied Hazel, "I know what you mean and I like you for that."

They all held hands around the table, and then after a moment of thought for absent Jimmy, moved off down to the theatre to see that night's show.

"Hey, there's a mind reader on tonight," said Burt, quite excited, "just like you see on the television!"

"Well mind you don't get involved, Burt old lad," added Linda, "we don't want showing up with what he sees in your mind, do we?"

Burt looked disappointed as he had visions of making this bloke look a fool with a bit of fooling about, but laughed it off and promised not to say anything. As if?

The ship was steaming away from Crete on the last part of the voyage, and everyone had enjoyed the cruise.

"It won't be long now before we're back in Athens," said Linda, "and then merry old England."

"Well, at least we've all had a good time and had a really good laugh," said Hazel.

"If only the children had been able to come with us though, wouldn't it have been great?" said Linda.

Hazel looked at Linda, and Linda looked at Hazel. Then they both agreed together, "Nah!"

"Listen at you two loving mothers," said Burt, "I'll tell them what you said when we get home!"

Linda jumped up from her deck chair, "Yes, you do Burt my lad and I'll throw you over the side right now!"

Just as the laughter was about to start again, Burt became wet through from a bucket full of water, which came from the deck above. This made the women cry with laughter, but as Burt was pulling his wet shirt away from his body, he looked up to see what was happening.

There was a lot of the crew carrying buckets of water and running to the end of the ship where the engine room was.

"I reckon something's wrong," said Burt, as the women stopped laughing and saw the seriousness of the situation. Black smoke was billowing from one of the funnels, and from out of two stairwells that led in the direction of the engine room.

"That doesn't look right to me," said Burt, very concerned, "I reckon the ship's on fire!"

"Oh no!" said Hazel, "don't let anything spoil this lovely holiday now."

The captain spoke over the tannoy system, "Attention, attention! Will all passengers go please to the front of the ship, where you will be told what to next do."

Burt and the women looked at each other, then decided that they ought to get some different clothes on and some personal items, just in case!

The three of them hurried down below to their cabin and got their passports, money and travel documents, wrapped them in a plastic bag and Burt put them inside his jacket pocket. Each of them wrapped a thick cardigan or jumper around their waist, to use later in case they were put into lifeboats. Although the weather was really hot during the day, it could turn very cold at night, especially on the sea. They made their way back up on the deck, and went to the front of the ship. Hundreds of people were standing near the rails, around the pool and at the front of all the deck levels, whilst the captain was still issuing his garbled message of hope.

All of a sudden there was a loud explosion from the rear of the ship and an even bigger blanket of black smoke went spiralling into the warm air. Quite a few women screamed and some children started crying, but

Burt, Hazel and Linda kept calm and waited to see what happened next.

The crew and staff of the ship started to remove the tarpaulins from the lifeboats and the captain gave the order to abandon ship.

"That's it!" said Burt. "Let's get off this bus before the last stop!"

"What's the last stop?" asked Linda.

"The bottom of the sea!" said Burt as he ushered them along the deck to the stairs that led to the lower deck.

It was no use; it was blocked tight with people who had the same idea. The two women were starting to panic and worry, but Burt kept them going to the next stairwell, and up to a higher deck, near the back of the ship. One of the crew came to help with a lifeboat, his face black with smoke, and his clothes smelling of fire.

"How bad is it?" asked Burt.

"Bad," he replied, "and to make it worse, this Greek crew didn't get the water-tight doors closed in time, in their panic, and now the ship's sinking fast!"

By the time they had managed to get the ropes ready for lowering, about one hundred people swarmed around them, pushing and shoving, fighting for a place in the boat. Hazel hung onto Linda who tried to hang onto Burt, but it was very hard to keep hold.

"Let's go to the next boat," shouted Linda.

"Get in this one, quickly!" shouted Burt to the two women, as he hung onto the side. Linda scrambled in, but someone pushed Burt from behind and he let go of Hazel's hand as he fell headlong into the boat.

Hazel watched as the boat slid away and down into the ocean. Burt was lying in the bottom of the boat, and Linda was shouting his name.

"I'll get the next boat!" shouted Hazel. "Don't worry, I'll see you later! Be careful and look after yourselves!"

Linda shouted Hazel's name a couple of times before they disappeared around the front of the ship, in a swarm of boats and people swimming. Every kind of item on board that would float had been thrown overboard, and people were clinging to anything that they could get hold of to keep afloat. It was quite frightening for Hazel, alone now, still being pushed and shoved by hundreds of people trying to get off the ship.

Then came a second loud explosion and the ship listed slightly to one side. The people began to panic even more, and screams could be heard all over the ship. Black smoke and flames were now pouring out of the rear end of the ship, and from stairwells and portholes along something like half its length.

Hazel walked quickly to the other side of the ship, looking for another boat, but they had all gone. Short of jumping into the sea there was no other way of escape, but when she looked over the edge from the second deck, it was a long way down!

The only people left on board were some older people who hadn't made it to the boats, and one or two of the crew. The rest of the crew and the captain had commandeered one of the first lifeboats, and were safely off the ship.

There was no need to rush about now. There didn't seem like much choice for Hazel now, she could either wait until somebody came to rescue her and be lifted off, or wait till the ship sank closer to the sea and jump in. There was the constant sound of small explosions, the shattering of glass and the rumbling of moving furniture. Hazel sat on a seat at the door to the dining hall, trying to think of a way to get off, just hoping and praying that someone would come! The ship hadn't listed any further, but was starting to sink evenly from end to end.

Hazel looked around at some of the people still trapped on board with her. They were still finding flotation devices and jumping over the rail, but most of them were elderly, invalid people who just sat on benches, weeping. There was no sign of Burt and Linda, but Hazel lived in the hope that they had made it to safety. Most of the boats had moved away from the ship in case it pulled them under when it sank. One or two were still picking up survivors from the water, but all the boats were vastly overcrowded.

An old woman came and sat by Hazel, weeping and asking if she had seen her husband. Hazel told her no, she hadn't seen anyone that fitted the description. The old woman moved on along the deck. Hazel walked slowly down the stairs to the ballroom bar, as there was a sun deck near there which she could probably get off from when it was nearer to the sea. She sat on a seat near the window, watching with tears in her eyes that started to roll down her cheeks. "If anyone comes now I'll see them," she thought, "and I can wave my cardigan so that they see me." The beautiful calm sea that she had loved to cruise over was now going to take her and her friends away. The lovely ship with all its fun and enjoyment had become her death trap and burial place, unless some form of rescue arrived very soon.

Andrew's little alarm system began to ring like a small egg timer. "Goodness me!" he shouted. "Jimmy, get back to me immediately!"

A fraction of a second passed and Jimmy arrived with another client.

"What's the panic now?" said Jimmy, expecting another one of Andrew's little grovelling routines, so that he would take on something strange or desperately urgent.

"Jimmy, it's Hazel's time, nearly," spluttered Andrew, "I nearly missed it, but she's not gone yet!"

"What's ... where ... I mean, where is she, Andrew?" stuttered Jimmy.

Andrew showed him the location and gave him a quick and very brief account of the situation so far.

"She's on her own and the rescue won't happen for some hours, but she's building up to a stroke with the strain of things. She needs someone to be with her, Jimmy, she needs you more than any time in her life! Go and do the best stage management job that you have ever done, my friend, and know that we are all with you! Go! Go now!"

Jimmy beamed down to the ship and saw the smoke and flames, the listing vessel sinking slowly into the deep ocean. People were still running back and forth trying to find relatives and friends, and some of the less fortunate were laid on the decks, dead.

By this time, Hazel had decided to go back to her cabin and see if there was anything that she ought to have with her, when the rescue boats finally came and took her off. She sat alone in the quietness, looking at her belongings, and those of Burt and Linda's. "What a tragic end to such a lovely holiday," she thought, "I hope that they got to safety." The tears began to roll down her cheeks as she fell sideways onto the bed, and sobbed.

There was a knock on the cabin door, which brought her quickly back to some sort of consciousness. As she got up to answer it, the door opened and there stood Jimmy. He was wearing the same old clothes that he used to wear for work, tweed jacket, brown trousers and shoes, checked shirt and blue tie.

"Hazel," he said, in his normal, loving voice.

"Jimmy?" replied Hazel. "Is it really you?"

"Aye lass, who else did you expect at your cabin door?"

"Oh Jimmy," screamed Hazel as she went quickly over to him and hugged him, with tears rolling down her face and onto his jacket.

He shut the door and led her to the bed, where they sat down side by side.

"Jimmy, is it going to end like this?" asked Hazel. "Am I going to die here or will I be rescued and saved? Tell me Jimmy, what's going to happen?"

"Well, it's like this sweetheart, the rescue boats are on the way, but they won't get here until it's too late for you, my dear," replied Jimmy. "You see, all this has been too much of a strain for you, and I don't think anyone would disagree that, being on a ship in the middle of the ocean, on fire and sinking, wouldn't make their hearts pound a lot harder than usual, do you see?"

"I have been scared senseless, Jimmy, until you came," said Hazel. "I had nobody to help me or be with me, and I was scared, Jimmy."

"Well I'm here now, love, if that's any comfort to you, as really, I've come to take you with me, in a short while," said Jimmy.

"Oh Jimmy, I always wanted to be with you, but now you've told me it's time, I'm frightened!" replied Hazel.

"Don't be, my love, it will be alright, you'll see," said Jimmy, as he put his arm around her and held her close. Hazel sobbed again and Jimmy tried to dry her eyes with a handkerchief that he just happened to have in his pocket.

They sat together for about fifteen minutes while Hazel tried to come to terms with the situation, cried and stopped, and cried again. Jimmy told her about things that she was going to see, people and friends, Andrew, and tried to explain that it was a completely different world, so to speak.

Jimmy took hold of her hands, leaned forward and kissed her tenderly. Hazel responded, and held the kiss for a few moments. It was like something that she hadn't felt since their courting days, and she liked it.

"How do you feel, my love?" asked Jimmy, quietly and in a loving way.

"I feel like we're courting all over again, Jimmy," replied Hazel, "you haven't kissed me like that for years."

"I haven't been around for years," replied Jimmy, with a smirk on his face.

"You know what I mean!" snapped Hazel in a sort of abrupt but loving voice. "It's been some time since we've been alone together."

"How do you feel, then?" asked Jimmy.

"I feel really strange, as if a burden has been lifted from me, and I'm not scared anymore!" replied Hazel.

"Well, that was it," said Jimmy.

"That was what?" replied Hazel.

"That was it, that was the kiss of death for you," said Jimmy, cautiously.

"The kiss of death?" asked Hazel. "But I'm not dead, I'm sitting here with you, aren't I?"

Jimmy looked her straight in the face, smiled a little, and then pointed to the bed at the side of her. There she could see her body, laid on her side, as if she had just fallen sideways onto the bed.

"JIMMY!" shouted Hazel. "What's happened? Why can I see myself lying on the bed beside me?"

"Because, my love, that is your dead body, and now you are a spirit," replied Jimmy, "now you are like me. It wasn't painful, was it?"

"When did that happen? I didn't feel a thing, and yet I thought that when I died it would hurt!" replied Hazel, somewhat alarmed.

"It happened when I kissed you, my love," said Jimmy, "that was the kiss of death, from the Angel of Death, Jimmy De'Ath, do you understand now?"

She hugged him and kissed him again, just to see what happened, and nothing did except, that it felt good.

"Jimmy, I'm dead, and I don't feel anything," said Hazel, with a perplexed frown on her face.

"What did you want to feel?" asked Jimmy, shrugging his shoulders, "a pain through your chest or something, I can arrange that if you really want?"

"No, no, it's just that, when you think of dying, you usually associate it with great pain, and I didn't feel anything," said Hazel.

"Some people don't," replied Jimmy, "and I had to make it easy for you, didn't I?"

"You have always thought so much about me, and I love you, Jimmy," said Hazel.

"Wow!" said Jimmy, "we always fancied a cruise didn't we? I never knew that these ships were as posh as this!"

"It's been marvellous, Jimmy," said Hazel, "up until now and all this happening. By the way, do you know if Burt and Linda are safe?"

"Yeah," replied Jimmy, "I thought you'd be worried so I checked on them on the way here. They've got into a lifeboat and will be picked up in about an hour."

"Thank God for that," she replied.

"Well, yes, I suppose you could, really," said Jimmy with a smile. "Are you going to give me a guided tour of the ship, then?"

"I suppose it wouldn't hurt to have one last look around," said Hazel, quite unconcerned as to what was happening to the ship.

By this time, there was a large cloud of black smoke billowing from the rear end of the ship, so Hazel made her way towards the bows, and showed Jimmy the bridge.

"Wow, lass," said Jimmy, I've always wanted to see what it was like in the driving seat of one of these big ships," as he took the wheel and gave it a few turns either way.

"You should see the magnificent ballroom where we danced every night away," said Hazel, turning Jimmy's attention away from the wheel and the many knobs and switches, clocks and dials.

"Well! Don't just stand there, let's have a gander at it then," said Jimmy.

The two of them made their way down the steps and corridors, three decks down to the ballroom.

Jimmy stepped inside the doors, his mouth fell open in disbelief.

"Bloody, bloody, blood ..." said Jimmy as Hazel stopped him short.

"Jimmy!" screamed Hazel, "Where on earth did you learn such bad language?"

"Sorry, lass," said Jimmy, with a finger on his bottom lip, "you tend to pick things up in this job, pardon the pun. Oh goodness, there, I said that phrase again!"

"Well, this was our table every night," said Hazel as she led Jimmy across the floor to where she spent each night with Burt and Linda.

"I bet that was something else, gliding across this beautiful dance floor, all poshed up like a dog's proverbial," said Jimmy.

"Yes, it was," answered Hazel, rather sadly, "and now it's all over and finished."

"Reminds me of our early days at the Coalville Palais," said Jimmy, "how about you?"

"Yes, my feet can still recollect being trodden on so many times that they can't forget it," replied Hazel with a smile. She looked around at the deserted place, so magnificent, yet so empty and lifeless.

"These places feed on the emotions that they create from people," said Jimmy, "and it's strange how lifeless they become when there's no life in them."

"Jimmy," replied Hazel, "where did you learn such profound knowledge like that? I've never known you to be so philosophical in your entire life!"

"It just pops out now and again," replied Jimmy, casually.

Whilst Hazel had her back turned to Jimmy, looking across the ballroom, she heard him say in his quiet, loving voice, "Excuse me young lady, would you do me the honour of the next dance, please?"

As she turned, she started to say, "What dance? There's no music, no people, no atmosphere, it's just a doomed, sinking ..." and then she saw Jimmy looking at her. He was dressed in the full evening dress of a captain, white from head to toe, and gold braid hanging from one of his epaulettes, gold stripes on his sleeves, and around the brim of his white cap.

Hazel stood transfixed for a moment, speechless.

"Well?" asked Jimmy.

"You look like that bloke on the films, Steven Seagal, only more handsome, and you're all mine!" gasped Hazel, still a little speechless.

"Just one thing, young lady" said Jimmy, "you're hardly likely to be the 'Belle of the Ball' in your woolly cardigan, are you?"

Hazel looked down and saw her clothes, the ones that she had on when she was waiting on the deck for help.

"Jimmy!" she said. "I wouldn't go to the supermarket dressed like this, how can I dance around this place like this?"

"No matter," said Jimmy, as he took her hand, and immediately she was changed into a glittering, gold ball gown, with diamonds around her neck and wrists, and the same dancing shoes that she wore at the Coalville Palais.

She looked at herself, with open mouth, and disbelief.

"Jimmy Coney! What have you done? It's beautiful!" was all she could manage to get out of her mouth.

"It's all part of the job," said Jimmy, with a wry smile. "All part of making it easy for you."

"Hey Andrew, what's happening? I heard that Jimmy, my buddy had been recalled, and urgent?" asked Danno.

"Yes, it's his wife's time and she was alone on a cruise ship, so he's gone down to do his best stage managing job on her," replied Andrew.

"Can I go, too?" asked Danno. "I could be of help to my buddy?"

"Well, I suppose ..." said Andrew before he was cut off by the disappearance of Danno and a few chosen souls that were around at the time! Twelve of the controllers also disappeared with him, to have a look at the big duo in action, first hand!

Andrew shook his head in amazement, "They could watch everything from here if they wanted to and no one ever enjoyed this job at all until Jimmy arrived."

There was a loud bang from behind the bar, and both of them looked with fear, thinking that part of the ship was breaking up. But it wasn't. A head appeared, then the big shoulders and grinning face of Danno, pouring champagne into three glasses all at once.

"Hi there good buddy," was his greeting, "and a special hello to the good lady Coney, I hope you are enjoying the Jimmy Coney School of Stage Managed Retrievals? Hey Jimbo, you didn't do her justice with that old photograph you showed me."

"Danno, what are you doing here?" asked Jimmy, somewhat amazed at seeing him.

"Hey buddy, Andy baby told me what was going down, the ship, pardon the pun ... oops! So I asked if I could come and help," said Danno, all excited at the chance of another adventure with Jimmy.

"Oh all right, good to see you anyway, and you have great timing as I've only just brought Hazel over to us," said Jimmy.

Hazel looked on in amazement as these two friends talked about death like it was, well, everyday stuff.

They quaffed a few glasses of champagne, and then Danno asked about Jimmy's plans.

"I have only one plan, my friend, buddy Danno," replied Jimmy "and that is to glide this young lady across the floor of this magnificent ballroom to the sound of the best big band in the after-world."

"Jimmy, you keep saying 'young' and you know how old I am," said Hazel, rather embarrassed, "and what's this about an old photograph?"

"Oh, take no notice of him, he's only trying to get you going, having a laugh," said Jimmy, as he took her to one of the large mirrors on the wall and showed her what she looked like. Hazel was amazed to say the least. She was a dazzling woman of something like thirty years old in the most luxurious dress that anyone had ever seen.

"Jimmy!" exclaimed Hazel. "What has happened to me?"

"When you're with the spirits, you don't age, we don't count time any more, and you don't have to be the old person that you were when you died," replied Jimmy, hand gestures to match his words.

Hazel couldn't get over how she looked; she was a young woman again! And Jimmy looked younger than when he died, too!

"Hey buddy," asked Danno, with his face and eyes pleading for Jimmy's approval before he asked the question.

"Yes, Danno, what is it?" said Jimmy, with a look of expectancy on his face.

"I've always wanted to lead one of those big bands, like in the fifties, can I ..."

"Danno, I wouldn't have it any other way, let's get this party moving, and bring on the band!" said Jimmy, as he whisked Hazel onto the floor.

The lights all came on. A band appeared on the stage, all dressed in the glittery uniform of a fifties swing band, including Danno of course, who lapped up every second of it. The music started and more people appeared on the dance floor. Jimmy swung Hazel around and around, looking like the dashing captain, with his beautiful lady in his arms.

"Where did you learn to dance so well?" asked Hazel, as Jimmy sped around the floor and twirled and waltzed her.

"When you're on this side, you can do anything, and all the things that you couldn't do before, you can do easily," replied Jimmy.

"But what if anyone comes, the rescue boats for instance, what will they say?" asked Hazel in a worried voice.

He called out to Danno as they glided past the front of the stage, "Hey Buddy, where did all the musicians come from anyway?"

"I did like you taught me," replied Danno, "I brung 'em with me from the office!"

Hazel danced and danced, twirling around Jimmy, and watching his beautiful dancing moves.

"You dance like a professional, Jimmy."

"I can do anything like a professional now, dear."

The band played on, and Jimmy and Hazel sat through some of the numbers, while Danno conducted his band, turning round occasionally and smiling at them.

"He's enjoying every minute of this, just look at him," said Jimmy.

"So am I, Jimmy," said Hazel, "but when does it all end, and the rescuers get here?"

"For you my love, the rescuers are here, and this is just the beginning," replied Jimmy, "and there's no end to your stamina, or what you can have or do, or where you can go, or who you can meet, it's just … Heaven! Of course, if you want to, you might even meet superstars like that bloke over there who's conducting the band, the one that we're not dancing to."

"Well, come on then, 'Jimbo' let's get going!" said Hazel.

"Come on Jimbo, Hazel, this is a special tune I'm playing just for you," shouted Danno.

"What's it called, Danno?" shouted Hazel.

"Crazy! Just suits the pair of you," said Danno, with his usual big grin on his face.

"How can you not like a bloke like him, Hazel?" said Jimmy.

"I feel like I've known him all my life," replied Hazel, as they danced around the room and up onto ceiling. Danno looked up as they danced across the ceiling above him and then all around the lights and glitter ball before settling back down onto the floor again. As they swirled around they were joined by something like fifty more couples, who danced alongside Jimmy and Hazel, full of smiles and greetings. As Jimmy neared the stage he called out to Danno, "Hey buddy, where's all this lot come from? Is this your doing?"

Danno shook his head and shrugged his shoulders, as if he was as surprised as Jimmy. Then one of the musicians stood up to play a solo piece of the tune, a little man with a balding head and silvery hair. He looked to be about six hundred years old, give or take a decade. The music was first class, and after he had finished playing the dancers clapped vigorously.

"That's Andrew, isn't it?" asked Hazel.

"Yeah, he's getting into this kind of thing now," replied Jimmy, "and I bet it was him who brought all this lot down to dance with us."

The music ceased and Danno brought his solo musician to the front of the stage. Everyone clapped their hands again as Andrew took a bow, and then made an announcement over the microphone.

"Ladies and Gentlemen, Captain Coney and honoured guest Hazel," said Andrew, "there will be people arriving soon to take care of the living, so we must all depart, pardon the pun, and go back to our respective places. Danno, thank you for your music, and all of you who enjoyed the dance, thank you and good night."

With that, the voice of the big boss, the room was instantly emptied, the lights went out, the band disappeared and all that was left was Jimmy, Hazel and Danno standing at the doorway of the ballroom.

"Hey buddy," asked Danno, "where have you left Hazel's old body, somewhere that it can be found easily?"

"Yeah," replied Jimmy, "it's in her cabin and I've left the door wide open. There was a crew member checking that deck anyway, earlier."

"You talk about me as though I wasn't here, you two!" said Hazel.

"Sorry dear," said Jimmy, as they linked arms with Danno on her left and Jimmy, back in his usual clothes, on her right.

"Hey Jimbo" said Danno, "doesn't this remind you of that film *The Wizard of Oz*, where they all go off, dancing up the yellow brick road?"

Jimmy looked at Danno with his usual look of 'don't start anything else' but it was too late, Hazel agreed with Danno's eye contact and the three of them had to act out the scene. They hadn't been singing for long before Danno was trying to fit some different lyrics into the song.

He was trying to include 'We're off to see Andrew' but he couldn't make the words fit in properly.

"What about, we're off to Andy baby's," suggested Jimmy.

"Yeah, buddy, I like that," agreed Danno and he started to fit it into the song.

When they arrived at Andrew's place, he was wearing a frown as they came face to face with him.

"Hey, buddy, I'm sorry, it was only a bit of fun with Jimbo and the missus, you know," stuttered Danno.

"I don't like the name Andy, as you well know Mr Danno," said Andrew, and then his face changed back to his normal smiling self. He welcomed Hazel and gave her the re-training that she had to have. That took all of a split second, as did the guided tour of the place. Hazel couldn't believe her eyes at the marvellous things that she saw and heard, touched and smelled.

"It's a whole new world!" said Hazel to Jimmy.

"'Course it is, dear," agreed Jimmy, "but you can't come here until it's the right time, like you have come here now."

"Can I see if Linda and Burt are all right? Did they get rescued in time?" asked Hazel.

Andrew drew her across to a large kind of screen and showed her Burt and Linda climbing aboard an aeroplane at Athens. They looked very well after their ordeal, though a little sad in their faces.

"Why are they looking so sad when they're on their way home and safe?" asked Hazel.

"Because they have had to identify the body of a woman, found in their cabin," replied Andrew.

"Oh!" said Hazel, "that'll be me won't it?"

"Afraid so," replied Andrew, "but at least your body will be sent back to England for a proper funeral, and that will give your family a chance to mourn over your passing."

"My family!" said Hazel, "I forgot all about them! What will they do without me, they'll be sad and missing me!"

"They will manage perfectly without you," said Andrew, "now that they have your body to bury, and they have your funeral arrangements to take care of. You managed all right when Jimmy crossed over, didn't you?"

"Well, yes," agreed Hazel, "there was so much to do, and it was no good worrying myself over it, it wouldn't have brought him back. I see what you mean, Andrew."

"Life goes on down there, no matter what happens," said Andrew, "whether it be death, disaster, fire or flood, they just get on with living again as soon as they can."

"Anyway, Andrew," piped up Jimmy, "when are you going to tell me what happened to Adolf Hitler, then?"

Hazel looked at Andrew, and Andrew at Hazel, and they both broke out into laughter.

"What?" said Jimmy. "What? Am I missing the point here or something?"

CHAPTER EIGHTEEN

Midsummer Madness

Jimmy had just returned to Andrew after visiting another level, where his mother and father were enjoying their well-earned rest.

"What's next then, boss?" asked Jimmy. "Where am I off to this time?"

"Well," replied Andrew, "you know how you used to like to go on those cheap holidays when you were alive?"

"Err ... yes," said Jimmy.

"Well, so do lots of other people, but I'm afraid that some of them don't appear to take the necessary precautions like you did."

"What do you mean?" asked Jimmy. "Like travel insurance and that sort of thing?"

"Oh no, much worse than that," said Andrew, "I mean important things like sun cream!"

"Sun cream?" said Jimmy. "Sun cream? Why is that more important than insurance?"

"You know about the rays from the sun, how they can be harsher in some places than others, and how people travel to hotter countries for a holiday," continued Andrew in his 'college professor' type of voice, "well, a lot of them think it's perfectly safe to lie on a beach all day without any protection from the sun."

"Well, where are these daft people?" asked Jimmy with a little amazement in his manner, after all, he would go and fetch souls from anywhere without any fuss.

"They're all over the world," replied Andrew, "and the numbers are increasing. But first I want you to go to the beach at Alcudia, in Majorca, there is a man there who is just about ready to cross over."

"I'm there," replied Jimmy, and he was.

Jimmy walked along the beach, dressed in shorts, tee shirt, socks and trainers. A nice pair of designer shades completed the look. He saw a man, lying face down on a large towel. His back was completely burnt and blistering in the heat, yet he didn't seem to know.

Jimmy walked over to him, "Hey mate, you all right?" he asked.

The man didn't acknowledge him at first, till Jimmy repeated his question.

"No," said the man, "I think I've been here a little too long and should turn over now, to get the other side done."

"I don't think you should," said Jimmy, "you're absolutely burnt to a cinder on your back, let me help you up and get some cream on it."

"Oh, I don't bother with that stuff," said the man, "you come all this way to get a tan and then they want you to put stuff on your skin to stop it from tanning!"

"It could save your life if nothing else," said Jimmy, a little sterner, "anyway, why do you want to go brown, what's wrong with white?"

"It's the done thing, isn't it?" retorted the man. "You go on holiday and come back brown so that everyone can see that you've had better weather than what they've had at home."

"Where are you from?" asked Jimmy.

"I come from Solihull, near Birmingham, England," replied the man. "Cold place at the best of times!"

"I thought I recognized your accent, I used to live somewhere near there," said Jimmy.

"God, my back does hurt you know, I think I'm going to have to get up for a while."

The man's spirit stood up alongside his red body, and looked around, and then at Jimmy.

"Who are you anyway, the life guard or something, and hey, who's that big red man laid there where I've been laid?"

"That, my friend is you!" said Jimmy sharply. "You've just about reached the point of no return and have just passed into a coma."

"How do *you* know all that?" asked the man, looking straight at Jimmy, bewildered.

"I know all this because I've now got the task of taking you across to the other side, if you happen to die, from all that blistering."

"That's me?" said the man. "But if that's me, how come I'm standing here talking with you?"

"Because I'm the Angel of Death who has come to take you across to the other side, that is, unless we can get some help for you," replied Jimmy.

"Angel of bloody death? You're having a laugh aren't you?" said the man. "I've never heard anything like it before in my life!"

"Well you won't be hearing anything like it again in your life if we don't get some help," replied Jimmy.

As the man watched, Jimmy walked through a sun lounger and a palm tree type of sun shade.

"There, now let's get moving and see if we can get you back into your body before it's too late!" said Jimmy.

The man nodded in some sort of agreement and waited for his next instruction. Jimmy saw a water hose wrapped around a pipe that was used as a beach shower, and went to see if he could make it reach to where the man's body was lying. It did, just, so he turned it on and sprayed some cold water over him to cool the skin down. The man looked on in amazement, as he could see what was happening, but couldn't feel the cold water. After a few minutes, the man began to sense something.

"Hey mate," he said, "I can feel something happening, I can feel a coldness coming over me, what's happening?"

"Hopefully," replied Jimmy, "it's the feeling of this cold water hitting your body, and you could return to the land of the living. If it's not ... well then, we're too late and you will have to come with me."

"You mean ... I'll be dead?" exclaimed the man.

"Afraid so," agreed Jimmy, "but let's hope that this works, first."

The man began to feel even colder as Jimmy washed over his body with the hose. Then, with a shriek, he disappeared back into his body.

"Thank God for that," said Jimmy.

"Yes, I suppose you could," came Andrew's voice, "or you could thank Jimmy De'Ath my Angel of Death for his quick thinking."

"Sorry Andrew, I just thought that if I could ..."

"Don't apologize, my friend," said Andrew, "it is always better to save a life than take one."

"Yes but ..." protested Jimmy.

"No yes buts, it's the way He wants it done. No longer just taking souls but rather, trying to prevent people from coming over prematurely," replied Andrew. "From now on, always do your best to prevent a death, just like you always try to do."

"Thanks mate," said Jimmy, "but what about this chap, then? What do I do next for him?"

"Go to the nearest hotel, that's where he's staying, and get them to help you," said Andrew.

Jimmy didn't walk across the beach, there was no time for that, he was immediately in the reception of the hotel. The receptionist smiled and asked if she could help. Jimmy told her to get an ambulance, quickly, as one of their guests was lying on the beach, in danger of dying from the sun.

She called someone on the phone, and a security man arrived in a couple of minutes.

"What seems to be the problem, sir?" he asked.

"One of your guests is lying out there on the beach, and he's been there too long. If we don't get some help, quickly, he will die from sun stroke," said Jimmy.

"Are you a doctor?" asked the security man, "How do you know that he is dying? How do you know that he is one of our guests?"

"Because I have just tried to revive him, and NO I'm not a doctor!" shouted Jimmy. "Now can we get an ambulance here, pronto!"

"I'm sorry, we cannot call out an ambulance unless we are certain that he is from this hotel, as you can realize, we would be calling ambulances for everyone," replied the security man.

"If he says that this bloke is from here, believe him!" said a voice from behind. It was Alan, the security man from the television centre in Nottingham. He heard the noise and came to see what was going on.

"This is Mr Coney, I know him. I work for his son in England. If you don't get a move on with this ambulance, we'll be calling one for you, bastard!" said Alan.

"Alan, good to see you again, I didn't think that you would remember me from such a long time back?" said Jimmy, as they waited for some action.

"You did me a great favour, getting rid of that bastard McGuire, and when your son took over it was a different place to work," replied Alan. "Everyone gets on with each other and we all have the greatest admiration for Gerry's work. Look at me, head of security and now I'm able to bring the wife on a holiday abroad for the first time."

"My son did all that?" asked Jimmy?

"Sure did! Sorted out the whole department and nearly the whole of the television industry. He's a good bloke, your son."

He turned to see his wife and their ten-year-old boy coming towards them.

"Here's the missus and the kid, we're off to the beach for an hour before dinner. Nice seeing you again, Mr Coney, I'll tell Gerry that I've bumped into you."

"Right! Thanks, see you again sometime, Alan," called Jimmy.

"Wait a minute!" thought Jimmy, "what am I saying, if he tells Gerry that he's spoken to me on his holidays, he'll wonder what's going on!"

"Don't worry, Jimmy," said Andrew, "they already think that you're getting around a bit."

"It's alright for you to say, but what are they going to think? I'm supposed to be dead, and I keep popping up all over the place!"

"Well, at least they won't have time to forget you!" said Andrew, laughing a little.

The ambulance finally arrived, and Jimmy took them to the man on the beach who, for some unknown reason was still alive! They picked him up and carried him away to the ambulance, before speeding off.

Jimmy went back to the hotel and arrived at the reception in time to hear the receptionist say, "Oh, this man will tell you what you want to know," and pointed in Jimmy's direction. There was a woman asking about her husband, and she spoke in a Brummy accent. Jimmy guessed right away who she was, it was the wife of the man on the beach.

"Do you know what's happened to my husband?" she asked.

"Yes, they've taken him to hospital with severe sun stroke, he's been laid on the beach for hours and was in a bad way when I found him," said Jimmy.

"Oh, I wonder where they've taken him, do you know?" she asked.

"Yes, but if you get a taxi outside they'll take you straight there."

"Oh, I daren't go in a taxi on my own, will you come with me?"

"Well ..." stuttered Jimmy.

"You can take our courtesy car, Mr Coney, if that's better for you and Mrs Peterson."

She threw Jimmy a bunch of keys with a registration number on them, and he escorted his new friend outside. He found the car easily, in fact, you couldn't miss it with the hotel's name splashed all over it in big letters – SUNWING.

Jimmy drove to the hospital, even though he didn't know where it was, and chatted with a woman that he had only just met.

"You on holiday too, then?" asked Mrs Peterson.

"Sort of. Yes I suppose you could say that," replied Jimmy.

"What sort of job have you got back home, then?" she asked.

"Well, I suppose you could say that I was retired, but I used to work for a company that laid gas pipes," replied Jimmy.

"My son worked on a pipe gang."

"Did he? In the Birmingham area?"

"Yes, but the silly bugger blew himself up one day. Silly bugger lit a fag up while they were digging some trench and laying gas pipes."

Jimmy couldn't believe it! This was the mother of Freddy the Fag, who he'd already brought over after the accident that she'd just mentioned. That means that the old boy on the beach was Freddy's father, and that he was just about as daft as Freddy!

"Yes," continued Jimmy, "I knew your son, I was his manager."

"Was you?" replied the woman, amazed. "You knew my son then?"

"Yes, always had to keep telling him about the fags and smoking on the job," said Jimmy.

"Just like his father," she replied, "and he's only in this mess now because he thinks he's got to go home brown! Daft bugger, I'll end up losing him as well at this rate."

"He'll be all right, don't worry, they know how to treat this sort of thing over in these hot countries," said Jimmy.

"I hope you're right," she replied, "I can't afford to loose him now, he's all I got after Freddy went."

Jimmy parked the car and Mrs Peterson went inside. A few minutes went by before she came hurrying out again to find Jimmy, who was just about to start away and return the car.

"Hey, wait a minute!" she shouted.

Jimmy stopped and got out of the car, "What's up lass?" he asked.

"They only speak Spanish in there, and I can't find out where my Bert is!"

She was in a right panic, so Jimmy escorted her back inside and went to the reception desk. He asked them about her husband, Mr Peterson, and asked where he had been taken. Of course, Jimmy could speak any language that he needed to, and the Spanish flowed like gas through a pipe.

Mrs Peterson was very impressed, and vowed to make sure everyone knew when she got home. Jimmy took her to her husband's bedside in a small side ward. There lay Bert Peterson, looking like a giant lobster and sore!

She began by asking him how he felt and then laced into him with some choice words mixed with lots of swearing. Jimmy excused himself, and told her that there were plenty of taxis at the hospital.

"Just tell them 'Sunwing Hotel' and give them six euros for the fare," he said, in between her shouting.

He took the car back to the hotel and told them that she had found him. Then he walked out of the doors and back to the beach.

"Who's next, Andrew, while I'm on beach patrol?" said Jimmy.

Andrew gave him a list of twenty more on that beach alone. Each one of them might be saved by getting them indoors or covered up right away.

"Strange this, you know," said Jimmy, "nobody ever told me that an angel patrolled the beach in the Med!"

"We've never had such a useful angel for decades, and before that, nobody did this sort of thing. They stayed in Rome or wherever," replied Andrew.

"Feeling a bit like 'Bay Watch' are you?" said Andrew with a gentle laugh.

"You betcha, mate," replied Jimmy, taking up the challenge of Andrew's humour, "all I need now is Danno and somebody drowning in the sea. That will make my day!"

From there, Jimmy translated himself to a little island, just off the coast of the Dominican Republic called Turks and Caicos Island. It was quite a beautiful part of the world, where Jimmy had once planned to go, but changed his mind.

"Give me the directions, Andrew," he said, as he climbed aboard a high-powered luxury boat. Of course, it didn't really exist, but it was what was required to do the next job successfully. Jimmy sped away from the dock and out to sea. There was a small motor launch that was being used for fishing trips, which had caught fire and was sinking. If Jimmy could get there quickly he could save all the five people on board. As the boat roared across the calm sea, Jimmy noticed that there were plenty of sharks about in the water.

"I hope they don't try and swim for the shore," said Jimmy.

"Sorry, my friend, but two have already tried and they're here. I'm afraid the sharks have had a feast," replied Andrew.

Jimmy felt sad at that report, until a loud voice began to sing from inside the cabin, and Jimmy heard the sound of someone coming through the cockpit door.

"How is my old buddy, Jimbo? The ghostest with the mostest!"

Jimmy turned to see the huge shape of Danno, face aglow, champagne in his hand.

"Danno, where did you spring from?" asked Jimmy.

"Andy baby thought that you might need some help and some cheering," replied Danno, "and here I am, buddy, at your command, captain Jimbo. It's just like old times again buddy, aint it?"

"I've just heard that two of my pick-ups have already crossed over after being eaten by sharks," said Jimmy, "so I'm not feeling really excited at the moment."

"Don't be down hearted, buddy, there is still the three that are clinging to the up-turned boat, they'll be more than glad to see us turn up. Especially with this bright baby of a boat! How do you get all these fantastic ideas to carry out your operations? I would never have thought of anything like this, or the Jumbo jet. I guess I would have just turned up in a dinghy and had them climb aboard, but not you, Jimbo, you've got flair and I love it!"

"Well, I suppose it comes with what you think will suit the situation best," replied Jimmy, feeling a little better for having been praised so much by his friend. "I just imagine what's needed and take it from there."

"You've certainly got some imagination, buddy!" said Danno. "Hey wait up a minute, I think I see the boat. Yes, it's there, look, Jimbo, steady as she goes and bring her around to the starboard side a little."

"That's new for a truck driver, isn't it, nautical talk?" said Jimmy, his humour beginning to return.

"Sure thing buddy, but when I get with you I just let myself go!" said Danno.

Jimmy held the boat steady whilst Danno helped the three men on board.

They were wet through and had a few stories to tell about sharks passing close to them. One of them asked if they had seen their other two friends who had started swimming for the shore, and Jimmy had to tell them the awful truth.

"How do you know that for sure?" asked one of the men.

"We saw the remnants floating in the water," replied Jimmy, very sorrowful.

Danno took them downstairs to the cabin and got them some dry clothes, which Andrew had thoughtfully provided. He made them some hot drinks and food, while Jimmy took a steady ride back to the island where they were staying.

"Hey Jimbo," said Danno, "do you have to take the boat back straight away, or can we have it for a little while longer?"

"Haven't you got any work to do?" replied Jimmy.

"Well, sure, but I didn't mean keep it for a century, like, just …"

"Of course we can have a little cruise around, I'm sure Andrew wouldn't mind," said Jimmy.

"Perhaps a little 'tea-break' would be a good idea, chaps," came Andrew's voice, "but wait for me and my friends."

"What?" said Danno.

Then Andrew appeared on deck, along with a date for Danno and Hazel, Jimmy's late wife.

"Hey this is cool, Andy baby, the real thing!" said Danno, all excited.

"Hello dear," said Jimmy, "it's nice to have you along with us again. What have you been up to since we last saw each other?"

"Jimmy my love, if you don't use your powers you will never guess where I've been," said Hazel.

"Here's your champagne," interrupted Danno as he pushed a couple of glasses their way.

"I've just been to a concert, and heard Elvis Presley singing, LIVE!" said Hazel.

Jimmy was stuck for words, he had forgotten that Hazel had always liked and bought records of Elvis Presley, and now she had heard him sing, in person!

"Jimmy, it was marvellous, and some other people did the backing, and I've heard all the other famous people too. I liked Jim Reeves, he was lovely!"

"Well," said Jimmy, "I'm a little bit gob-smacked lass, I never thought in my entire life that being dead would be so wonderful. I didn't like leaving you behind, but I didn't wish for you to come across too soon either. Now you're here, you're enjoying things as much as you did when we were alive!"

They hugged and kissed, and stood arm-in-arm while Jimmy steered the boat and sipped his champagne. Danno and the others were playing some music and chatting, until Andrew decided to have a go at dancing. Then the laughter broke out and was uncontrollable. Four more couples joined the boat, some being friends of Andrew and some friends of Jimmy's, when he was alive.

After a few hours of fun, Andrew called a halt to the party and bade them all a fond farewell. The boat vanished and everyone on it, leaving Jimmy and Danno on an empty beach.

"Guess that's it till another day, buddy," said Danno.

"Seems that way, mate, unless you fancy staying with me for a few more jobs?" replied Jimmy.

"Can't," said Danno, "got the whole of the Miami coastline to run down yet, and then I've got jobs piling up in Chicago."

"Aye, it's a busy old life isn't it?" said Jimmy.

"Catch up with you later, buddy, but if you ever need a hand with one of your big productions, don't hesitate to give me a call," said Danno, as he disappeared off the beach.

"Sure thing good buddy," said Jimmy, as he looked out to sea and thought of the three men that he had rescued, "I sure will buddy. You know, sometimes I think I'll wake up in bed one morning and find that this has all been some kind of weird dream."

"I don't think you will," said Andrew's voice, quietly, "this, my friend, is your reality now, and probably it can make you feel like your *life* was some kind of dream."

"Which one is the dream and which one is the reality? I ask myself," said Jimmy.

The End — or is it?